HODDER GCSE HISTORY FL

WEIMAR AND NAZI GERMANY

1918–39

Steve Waugh • John Wright

In order to ensure that this resource offers high-quality support for the associated Pearson qualification, it has been through a review process by the awarding body. This process confirms that this resource fully covers the teaching and learning content of the specification or part of a specification at which it is aimed. It also confirms that it demonstrates an appropriate balance between the development of subject skills, knowledge and understanding, in addition to preparation for assessment.

Endorsement does not cover any guidance on assessment activities or processes (e.g. practice questions or advice on how to answer assessment questions), included in the resource nor does it prescribe any particular approach to the teaching or delivery of a related course.

While the publishers have made every attempt to ensure that advice on the qualification and its assessment is accurate, the official specification and associated assessment guidance materials are the only authoritative source of information and should always be referred to for definitive guidance.

Pearson examiners have not contributed to any sections in this resource relevant to examination papers for which they have responsibility. Examiners will not use endorsed resources as a source of material for any assessment set by Pearson.

Endorsement of a resource does not mean that the resource is required to achieve this Pearson qualification, nor does it mean that it is the only suitable material available to support the qualification, and any resource lists produced by the awarding body shall include this and other appropriate resources.

Hachette UK's policy is to use papers that are natural, renewable and recyclable products and made from wood grown in sustainable forests. The logging and manufacturing processes are expected to conform to the environmental regulations of the country of origin.

Orders: please contact Bookpoint Ltd, 130 Milton Park, Abingdon, Oxon OX14 4SE. Telephone: +44 (0)1235 827720. Fax: +44 (0)1235 400454. Email education@bookpoint.co.uk Lines are open from 9 a.m. to 5 p.m., Monday to Saturday, with a 24-hour message answering service. You can also order through our website: www.hoddereducation.co.uk

ISBN: 978 1 4718 6191 8

© Steve Waugh, John Wright 2016

First published in 2016 by
Hodder Education,
An Hachette UK Company
Carmelite House
50 Victoria Embankment
London EC4Y 0DZ

www.hoddereducation.co.uk

Impression number   10 9 8 7 6 5 4 3 2

Year   2020 2019 2018 2017 2016

Cover photos © World History Archive/Alamy

Typeset in ITC Legacy Serif 10/12pt by DC Graphic Design Ltd

Artwork by DC Graphic Design Ltd, Tony Randell, Steve Smith, White-Thomson Publishing Ltd

Printed in Italy

A catalogue record for this title is available from the British Library.

CONTENTS

Introduction

About the course

During this course you must study four studies:

- A thematic study and historic environment
- A period study
- A British depth study
- A modern depth study.

These studies are assessed through three examination papers:

- For Paper 1 you have one hour and 15 minutes to answer questions on your chosen theme.
- In Paper 2 you have one hour and 45 minutes to answer questions on a depth study and a British period study.
- In Paper 3 you have one hour and 20 minutes to answer questions on one modern depth study.

Modern depth study (Paper 3)

There are four options in the modern depth study unit. You have to study one. The four options are:

- Russia and the Soviet Union, 1917–41
- Weimar and Nazi Germany, 1918–39
- Mao's China, 1945–76
- The USA, 1954–75: conflict at home and abroad.

About the book

The book is divided into four key topics:

- **Key topic 1** examines the Weimar Republic 1918–29, including the origins of the Weimar Republic, its early challenges, the extent of recovery under Stresemann and changes in society durng this period.
- **Key topic 2** explains Hitler's rise to power 1919–33, including the founding and growth of the Nazi Party, the impact of the Munich Putsch, the increased support in the years after 1929, the developments of 1932–33 which made Hitler Chancellor, and the impact of the Great Depression.
- **Key topic 3** concentrates on how Hitler created a Nazi dictatorship through the removal of opposition, the creation of a police state and the use of censorship and propaganda.

- **Key topic 4** examines life in Nazi Germany in the years 1933–39, including policies towards women and the young, employment and living standards, and the persecution of minorities.

Each chapter in this book:

- contains activities – some develop the historical skills you will need, others are exam-style questions that give you the opportunity to practise exam skills.
- gives step-by-step guidance, model answers and advice on how to answer particular question types in Paper 3.
- defines key terms and highlights glossary terms in bold and colour the first time they appear in each key topic.

About Paper 3

Paper 3 is a test of:

- knowledge and understanding of the key developments in Germany, 1918–39
- the ability to answer brief and extended essay questions
- the ability to answer source and interpretation questions.

You have to answer the following types of questions. Each requires you to demonstrate different historical skills:

- **Inference** – making two supported inferences.
- **Causation** – explaining why something happened and assessing the importance of these causes.
- **Utility** – evaluating the usefulness of sources.
- **Interpretation** – explaining what differences there are between two interpretations and why they differ. Making a judgement on a view given by one of the interpretations.

On page 5 is a set of exam-style questions (without the sources). You will be given step-by-step guidance throughout the book on how best to approach and answer these types of questions.

Paper 3: Modern depth study
Option 31: Weimar and Nazi Germany, 1918–39

This is an **inference** question – you have to make two inferences and support each with details from the source.

1 Give two things you can infer from Source A about the Reichstag fire of February 1933. Complete the table below to explain your answer.

   i)   What I can infer:

....

....

       Details in the source that tell me this:

....

....

   ii) What I can infer:

....

....

       Details in the source that tell me this:

....

....

(Total for Question 1 = 4 marks)

This is a **causation** question – which gives you two points. You should develop at least three clear points and explain the importance of each of them.

2 Explain why there was increased support for the Nazis in the years 1929–32.

> You may use the following in your answer:
> ■ Unemployment
> ■ Goebbels
>
> You **must** also use information of your own.

(Total for Question 2 = 12 marks)

This is a **utility** question – it is asking you to decide how useful each source is.

3 (a) Study Sources B and C. How useful are Sources B and C for an enquiry into the effects of Nazi policies towards women in the years 1933–39? Explain your answer, using Sources B and C and your knowledge of the historical context.

(8)

This is an **interpretation** question – you have to explain one main difference between the two interpretations.

(b) Study Interpretations 1 and 2. They give different views about the effects of Nazi policies towards women in the years 1933–39. What is the main difference between these views? Explain your answer, using details from both interpretations.

(4)

This is an **interpretation** question – you have to explain why these interpretations differ.

(c) Suggest one reason why Interpretations 1 and 2 give different views about the effects of Nazi policies towards women in the years 1933–39. You may use Sources B and C to help explain your answer.

(4)

Up to 4 marks of the total for part (d) will be awarded for spelling, punctuation, grammar and use of specialist terminology.

This is an **interpretation judgement** question – you are asked to make a judgement on a view given by one of the interpretations.

(d) How far do you agree with Interpretation 2 about the effects of Nazi policies towards women in the years 1933–39? Explain your answer, using both interpretations, and your knowledge of the historical context.

(20)

(Total for spelling, punctuation and grammar, and the use of specialist terminology = 4 marks)

(Total for Question 3 = 36 marks)

(Total for Paper = 52 marks)

KEY TOPIC 1 The Weimar Republic, 1918–29

This key topic examines the key developments in the Weimar Republic, from its inception and early challenges to its recovery under Gustav Stresemann. This was a time of despair and also great hope for Germany. At the beginning of the period it was thought that the country could accept a new democratic constitution, but the challenges the Republic faced during the period of chaos, violence and economic instability after the First World War called this into question. However, by the end of 1923 political and economic stability were being restored to Germany, and Weimar was not challenged during the period of prosperity that lasted until 1929.

Each chapter within this key topic explains a key issue and examines important lines of enquiry as outlined in the boxes below.

There will also be guidance on how to answer the interpretations question.

- Understanding interpretations (page 18)
- How to answer the first question on interpretations – what is the main difference between the views? (page 23)

CHAPTER 1 THE ORIGINS OF THE REPUBLIC, 1918–1919

- The legacy of the First World War: the abdication of the Kaiser, the Armistice and revolution, 1918–19.
- The setting up of the Weimar Republic. The strengths and weaknesses of the new Constitution.

CHAPTER 2 THE EARLY CHALLENGES TO THE WEIMAR REPUBLIC, 1919–23

- Reasons for the early unpopularity of the Republic, including the 'stab in the back' theory and the key terms of the Treaty of Versailles.
- Challenges to the Republic from left and right: *Freikorps*, the Spartacists and the Kapp Putsch.
- The challenges of 1923: hyperinflation, the reasons for and effects of the French occupation of the Ruhr.

CHAPTER 3 THE RECOVERY OF THE REPUBLIC, 1924–29

- Reasons for economic recovery, including the work of Stresemann, the Rentenmark, the Dawes Plan, the Young Plan and American loans and investments.
- The impact on domestic policies of Stresemann's achievements abroad: the Locarno Pact, joining the League of Nations and the Kellogg–Briand Pact.

CHAPTER 4 CHANGES IN SOCIETY, 1924–29

- Changes in the standard of living including wages, housing, unemployment and insurance.
- Changes in the position of women in work, politics and leisure.
- Cultural changes: developments in architecture, art, and cinema.

TIMELINE

1918 November	Kaiser Wilhelm II abdicates	1924	Dawes Plan
1919 January	Spartacist uprising	1925	Locarno Pact
1919 June	Signing of the Treaty of Versailles	1926	Germany joins League of Nations
1919 August	Weimar Constitution finalised	1928	Kellogg–Briand Pact
1920	Kapp Putsch	1929	Young Plan
1923	French occupation of the Ruhr and hyperinflation		

1 The origins of the Republic, 1918–19

On 9 November 1918, Kaiser Wilhelm II abdicated the German throne and fled to Holland. Germany became a republic and, two days later, the Armistice was signed bringing an end to fighting in the First World War (1914–18). Within a few months a new republic with a new constitution was set up. This new constitution was in many respects one of the most democratic in the world with a president as the head of state. However, it also included several features which were to contribute to the instability, weakness and eventual downfall of the Weimar Republic, particularly proportional representation and Article 48 which gave powers to the president in an emergency.

1.1 The legacy of the First World War

The First World War had started in August 1914 and Europe was torn in two. Britain, France and Russia (the Allies) fought against Germany, Austria–Hungary and Turkey (the Central Powers). The USA joined the Allies in April 1917. By the early autumn of 1918, the German army was being pushed back on the Western Front in France, and the British naval blockade had resulted in shortages of food for the German people. German defeat was imminent.

In early October 1918, a new government was formed in Germany led by Prince Max of Baden. It included members of the Reichstag (parliament) and was Germany's first parliamentary cabinet. This meant that the government was accountable to the Reichstag rather than to the Kaiser (emperor). Up to this time, the Kaiser had had control over the army and navy as well as parliament.

The Revolution of 1918–19

Prince Max approached President Woodrow Wilson of the USA about ending the war but Wilson said that he would not discuss peace terms with Germany while the Kaiser and his military advisers were in control. Wilson insisted that they had to go. At the end of October 1918, the German navy mutinied. In the Kiel Mutiny, sailors at Kiel refused to put to sea and attack the British navy because they felt that such a move was foolish and might endanger the ceasefire talks. Unrest began to spread across Germany.

On 9 November, Kaiser Wilhelm, realising he now had little support, made the decision to abdicate. Two days later, the Chancellor of the newly declared German Republic, Friedrich Ebert accepted the Armistice on the basis of President Wilson's Fourteen Points (see box). It was assumed by all combatants that all states would be involved in the peace process. Ebert then announced that there would be elections for a Constituent Assembly on 19 January 1919.

> **The Fourteen Points**
> These were put forward by the American president, Woodrow Wilson, in January 1918 as a basis for the peace talks at Versailles. They included the idea of self-determination, which looked to give nations the right to rule themselves, as well as the establishment of a League of Nations which would guarantee freedom and preserve future peace.

ACTIVITIES

1 Read the text on this page and construct a timeline to show the steps towards the elections of a Constituent Assembly in January 1919.
2 Why did Kaiser Wilhelm abdicate in November 1918?
3 Study Source A. Why do you think Germany sent civilians and an ordinary army officer to sign the Armistice?

▲ **Source A** 'The signing of the Armistice'. This 1918 picture shows the Allied commanders receiving the German delegation before the signing of the Armistice. The Germans sent two civilians and an army officer

1.2 The setting up of the Weimar Republic

In the final weeks of 1918, Germany continued to experience tremendous upheaval and there were attacks on the new government from the left and the right. After the elections for the Constituent Assembly, it was decided that Berlin was too dangerous a place for the members to meet. Therefore, the decision was taken to meet in the more peaceful surroundings of the town of Weimar (hence the eventual name of the new Republic).

The most important result of the January elections was that no single party had a majority of seats (see Table 1.1). Therefore, there would have to be a coalition government.

The Assembly chose Friedrich Ebert of the Social Democratic Party (SPD) to be the new president. Ebert asked Philipp Scheidemann of the SPD to be Chancellor and form a government. Lacking a majority, Scheidemann formed a coalition with the Catholic Centre Party (ZP) and German Democratic Party (DDP). Because there were so many political parties it was difficult to secure an overall majority, and coalitions became a feature of the Weimar Republic.

The members of the Assembly had two key tasks before them. The first was the drawing up of a new constitution and the second was the formulation of a peace treaty with the Allies.

▼ Table 1.1 The results of the January 1919 elections

Party	No. of seats
Social Democratic Party (SPD)	163
German Democratic Party (DDP)	75
Centre Party (ZP)	71
German National People's Party (DNVP)	44
Independent Social Democratic Party of Germany (USPD)	22
Bavarian People's Party (BVP)	20
German People's Party (DVP)	19
Others	7

ACTIVITIES

For all of these questions, work in pairs.

1 What does Table 1.1 show about the results of the January 1919 elections?

2 Why was the Weimar Republic so named?

3 Why was a coalition government formed in 1919?

Source B Friedrich Ebert ▶ (centre) at a press reception in November 1919, the day he was elected President of the Weimar Republic

The Weimar Constitution

Following the abdication of the Kaiser, a new constitution had to be drawn up, which was finalised in August 1919. This was the first time that Germany had experienced democracy. Figure 1.1 shows how the constitution was organised, and Source C lists some of its key articles.

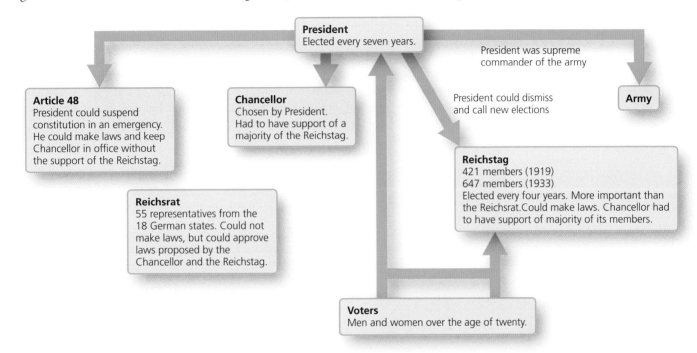

President
Elected every seven years.

President was supreme commander of the army

President could dismiss and call new elections

Army

Article 48
President could suspend constitution in an emergency. He could make laws and keep Chancellor in office without the support of the Reichstag.

Chancellor
Chosen by President. Had to have support of a majority of the Reichstag.

Reichstag
421 members (1919)
647 members (1933)
Elected every four years. More important than the Reichsrat. Could make laws. Chancellor had to have support of majority of its members.

Reichsrat
55 representatives from the 18 German states. Could not make laws, but could approve laws proposed by the Chancellor and the Reichstag.

Voters
Men and women over the age of twenty.

▲ Figure 1.1 The organisation of the Weimar Constitution

▼ Source C Key articles of the Weimar Constitution

Article 1	The German Reich is a republic. Political authority derives from the people.
Article 22	The Reichstag delegates are elected by universal, equal, direct and secret suffrage by all men and women over twenty years of age, in accordance with the principles of proportional representation.
Article 23	The Reichstag is elected for four years.
Article 41	The Reich President is chosen by the whole of the German electorate.
Article 48	If public safety and order in the Reich is materially disturbed or endangered, the Reich President may take the necessary measures to restore public safety and order.
Article 54	The Reich Chancellor and ministers require for the administration of their offices the confidence of the Reichstag. They must resign if the Reichstag withdraws its confidence.

ACTIVITY ?

Study Source C and Figure 1.1. In what ways was the constitution democratic and in what ways undemocratic? Complete your answer using a copy of the table below.

Democratic: Government in which all the people are involved in the decisions	Undemocratic: Government in which the people are not involved

Strengths of the new constitution

The new constitution had several strengths:

- In some ways the laws of the Weimar Republic were very democratic. Men and women had the vote at the age of 20, at a time when in Britain the age for men was 21 and 30 for women.
- The head of the government (the Chancellor) had to have the support of most of the people in the Reichstag.
- A strong president was necessary to keep control over government and to protect the country in a crisis.
- Voting by proportional representation meant that the number of seats each party had in the Reichstag was based on the number of votes they got. For example, if a party won ten per cent of the votes if was given ten per cent of the seats.

Weakness of the new constitution

There were, however, many flaws in the constitution and when things did not go well for Germany in the early post-war years, Ebert and his colleagues were criticised for creating a weak system of government (see Source D). Figure 1.2 shows some of the flaws of the new constitution.

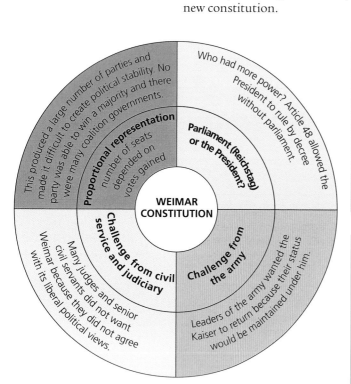

▲ Figure 1.2 Flaws of the Weimar Constitution

Source D From a speech to the new Constituent Assembly by Hugo Preuss, head of the Commission that drew up the Weimar Constitution in 1919. He was talking about the new constitution.

I have often listened to the debates with real concern, glancing timidly to the gentlemen of the Right, fearful lest they say to me: 'Do you hope to give a parliamentary system to a nation like this, one that resists it with every sinew in its body?' One finds suspicion everywhere; Germans cannot shake off their old political timidity and their deference to the authoritarian state.

ACTIVITIES

1. Make a copy of and complete the scales to show the strengths and weaknesses of the Weimar Constituton after reading the information on this page. Do you agree that the constitution made the Republic weak?

2. Sort the flaws of the Weimar Constitution (Figure 1.2) in order of importance in creating a weak government. Give reasons for your answer.

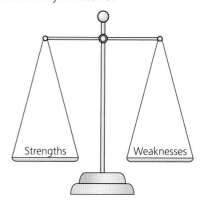

Practice question

Give two things you can infer from Source D about the Weimar Constitution. (For guidance, see page 78.)

2 The early challenges to the Weimar Republic, 1919–23

The setting up of the Weimar Republic did not signal peace for Germany and its citizens, it merely ushered in a period of chaos and violence. The five years after the First World War saw an attempted Communist revolution, political assassinations, putsches (armed uprisings) and massive inflation. Above all, Germans had to accept what they felt was a vindictive peace settlement – the Treaty of Versailles. Many Germans said that all the problems of the post-war years were the result of the decisions that had been made by the politicians of the new Weimar Republic. These politicians were given the name November Criminals. However, by the end of 1923, political and economic stability were being restored to Germany.

2.1 The early unpopularity of the Republic

The main reason for the early unpopularity of the Republic was the signing of the Treaty of Versailles.

The Treaty of Versailles

Although the Germans signed the armistice on 11 November 1918, it was not until 28 June 1919 that the treaty ending the First World War was signed. The Germans expected the peace settlement to be based on US President Wilson's Fourteen Points and they expected to return lands that they had conquered. However, they looked to President Wilson's idea of self-determination as a safeguard of Germany's sovereignty. When the terms of the settlement were published, huge numbers of Germans were horrified.

The French, led by Clemenceau, wanted revenge and sought to make sure Germany could never threaten France again. One British politician said that 'Germany will be squeezed until the pips squeak.'

The Treaty of Versailles imposed extremely severe terms on Germany (see Figure 2.1, and Table 2.1 on page 12). Germany lost 13 per cent of its land, 48 per cent of its iron production and more than 6 million citizens were absorbed into other countries. Perhaps the harshest term for Germany was Article 231 – the War Guilt Clause. This stated that Germany had to accept blame for starting the war in 1914. This was compounded when the treaty denied Germany entry to the League of Nations, thus showing that Germany was a pariah.

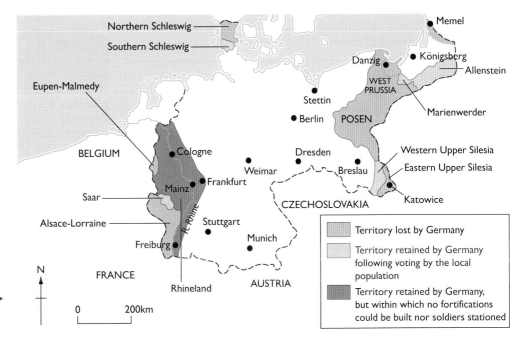

Figure 2.1 The territorial terms of the Treaty of Versailles

Territorial terms	Military terms	Financial terms
All colonies to be given to the Allied Powers	Army not to exceed 100,000	Coal to be mined in the Saar by France
Alsace-Lorraine returned to France	No tanks, armoured cars or heavy artillery permitted	Reparations fixed at £6.6 billion
Eupen-Malmedy given to Belgium after a plebiscite	No military aircraft permitted	Cattle and sheep to be given to Belgium and France as reparations
Saar to be administered by the League of Nations	No naval vessel to be greater than 10,000 tons	Ships over 1,600 tons to be given up
Posen and West Prussia to Poland. Eastern Upper Silesia to Poland after a plebiscite	No submarines permitted	Germany to build merchant ships to replace Allied ships sunk by U-Boats
Danzig created a Free City	Rhineland demilitarised	
Memel to be administered by the League of Nations		
No union (Anschluss) with Austria		
Northern Schleswig to Denmark after a plebiscite		

▲ Table 2.1 Some of the most important terms of the Treaty of Versailles

The 'stab in the back' theory

For most Germans, the Treaty stoked the fire of shame and humiliation. Versailles was nothing more than a dictated peace (*Diktat*). A scapegoat was needed – and Ebert, the Weimar Government and its politicians fitted the bill and people began to call them the November Criminals. Yet, there was much irony in this criticism. The German cabinet initially rejected the terms of the peace settlement and on 19 June 1919 Scheidemann resigned as Chancellor in disgust. Ebert called the terms a *Gewaltfrieden* (an enforced peace). The German public was unaware that the Allies had informed the German leaders that refusal to accept the terms would lead to a renewal of hostilities and an immediate invasion of Germany. Nevertheless, from this point, criticism of the Government began to grow and the idea that the politicians had stabbed the army in the back (the *Dolchstoss* theory) really took hold and gained currency.

▲ **Source B** A cartoon entitled 'Clemenceau the Vampire'. From the German right-wing satirical magazine *Kladderadatsch*, July 1919. Clemenceau was the leader of France. The cartoon is commenting about the Treaty of Versailles.

Source A From a German newspaper, *Deutsche Zeitung*, 28 June 1919

Vengeance! German nation! Today in the Hall of Mirrors [Versailles] the disgraceful treaty is being signed. Do not forget it. The German people will, with unceasing work, press forward to reconquer the place among nations to which it is entitled. Then will come vengeance for the shame of 1919.

ACTIVITIES

1 What does Source A show about the German newspaper's attitude to the peace settlement?

2 Why was Article 231 important for many Germans?

3 Work in groups of three or four. Choose either the territorial, military or financial terms of the Treaty of Versailles. Present a case for the class indicating that your choice had the most drastic consequences for Germany.

? Practice questions

1 Give two things you can infer from Source A about German reactions to the Treaty of Versailles. (*For guidance, see page 78.*)

2 How useful are Sources A and B for an enquiry into attitudes in Germany towards the Treaty of Versailles? Explain your answer using Sources A and B and your knowledge of the historical context. (*For guidance, see pages 62–64.*)

2.2 Challenges to the Republic from the left and right

At the same time that Ebert and Scheidemann were trying to establish a new government in Germany, there was political turmoil across the country. In its early years, the Weimar Republic faced constant threats from the left and right and there were several uprisings across Germany that threatened the existence of the Government (see Figure 2.2). It seemed that the Weimar Government could not win. Its politicians were criticised for ending the war, accepting the Treaty of Versailles and then introducing high taxes for the better off in society in order to meet the Allied reparations.

Firstly, it must be understood that the radical changes that occurred in Germany in late October and early November 1918 came about because those in power in Germany saw there was no alternative. Some Germans felt that democracy had been imposed on them. Furthermore, the consequences of the war were creating unrest in Germany. As a result of the British naval blockade, there were still shortages of food. Moreover, the German people were beginning to experience inflation. Add to these problems the impact of the Bolshevik Revolution in Russia, and it is easy to see why unrest spread.

Threat from the left

After the Bolshevik Revolution in Russia in October 1917, when the Provisional (temporary) Government was removed by the communists Lenin and Trotsky, many Germans hoped that a socialist country could be established in Germany as well. Soldiers, sailors and workers set up councils (soviets) in October and November 1918. Because of the fear of revolution, Ebert made a deal with the new army leader, Groener.

It was agreed that the army would support the new government against revolution and Ebert would support and supply the army. Thus the new government was dependent on the army, many leaders of which did not want democracy but preferred it to a Bolshevik style of government. For some Germans, this dependency on the army weakened the authority of the Weimar Republic.

ACTIVITIES

1 Why was there a fear of a Bolshevik Revolution in Germany?
2 Why was the deal between Ebert and Groener significant for the Weimar Republic?

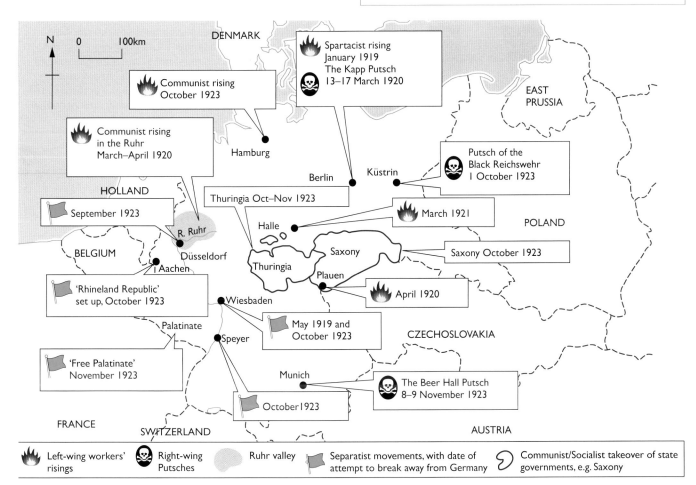

▲ Figure 2.2 Political violence in Germany, 1919–23

The Spartacist Uprising

During the war, several groups emerged from the German Social Democratic Party (SPD). The most radical was the Spartacist League led by Karl Liebknecht and Rosa Luxemburg, who eventually sought to establish a state based on communist ideals. (The League took its name from the Roman slave Spartacus, who led a rebellion in 73BC.) In December 1918, the Spartacists' demonstrations against the Government led to clashes with the army and resulted in the deaths of sixteen Spartacists. At the end of the month, the Spartacists formed the German Communist Party (KPD).

On 6 January 1919, the Spartacists began their attempt to overthrow Ebert and the Weimar Government in order to create a Communist State. Ebert and his defence minister, Noske, used the *Reichswehr* (regular army) and the Berlin *Freikorps* (see box) to put down the rebellion. Within days the rising was over. The Spartacists were no match for the army and *Freikorps*. Liebknecht and Luxemburg were captured and killed. It was the violence of the rising that forced the new Assembly to move to Weimar.

In March, a further communist-inspired rising in Berlin was put down with great ferocity and more than 1,000 people were killed. Another communist rising in Munich was crushed by the *Freikorps* with great severity in April.

> **Freikorps**
> Paramilitary groups formed from demobilised soldiers at the end of the war. They refused to give up weapons and uniforms and were led by ex-army officers. Most *Freikorps* were monarchists who sought to save Germany from Bolshevism even though they did not support the Weimar Republic. There were about two hundred different groups across Germany.

◀ **Source C** Photograph of *Freikorps* in front of the *Vorwarts* newspaper building, which they captured from the Spartacists in January 1919. The *Vorwarts* was a socialist newspaper

> **Source D From an article in a government newspaper, 1919**
>
> The despicable actions of Liebknecht and Rosa Luxemburg soil the revolution and endanger all its achievements. The masses must not sit quiet for one minute longer while these brutal beasts and their followers paralyse the activities of the republican government and incite the people more and more to civil war.

ACTIVITIES

1 Study Source C. Who were the Spartacists? Why was it important for them to control the *Vorwarts* building?
2 How did the Spartacists threaten the Weimar Republic?

Practice question

Give two things you can infer from Source D about the Spartacists. *(For guidance, see page 78.)*

The Kapp Putsch

Having resisted the challenge from the left, Ebert had to face the right in 1920. When the Weimar Government announced measures in March 1920 to reduce the size of the army and also disband the *Freikorps*, there was uproar in Berlin. The leader of the Berlin *Freikorps*, Ehrhardt, refused to comply. Together with a leading Berlin politician, Wolfgang Kapp, a plan was drawn up to seize Berlin and form a new right-wing government with Kapp as the Chancellor. Kapp stressed the communist threat, the *Dolchstoss* theory (see page 12) and the severity of the Treaty of Versailles. The *Reichswehr* in Berlin, commanded by General Luttwitz, supported Ehrhardt and Kapp. Following Kapp's successful seizure of Berlin on 13 March 1920, the Weimar Government moved to Dresden and then Stuttgart. The new regular army had been asked to put down the Kapp Putsch, but the Commander-in-Chief, von Seeckt, said 'The *Reichswehr* does not fire on *Reichswehr*.'

Ebert and Scheidemann called on the people of Berlin not to support the Kapp Putsch and asked them to go on strike. Trade unionists and civil servants supported the Government and, because it had little support, the Putsch collapsed. More than four hundred *Reichswehr* officers had been involved in the Putsch but very few were punished.

Further uprisings

One week after the Kapp Putsch began, a communist rising occurred in the Ruhr. This time the army became involved and brutally put down the rebellion. Hundreds were killed. Violence continued in Germany during the next two years and both left-wing and right-wing groups were involved.

It has been estimated that there were 376 murders (354 of them carried out by the right) in the period 1919–22. No right-wingers were sentenced to death but ten left-wingers were. Two leading Weimar ministers were assassinated during this time:

- In 1921, Matthias Erzberger, leader of the Centre Party and a signatory of the Treaty of Versailles.
- In 1922, Walther Rathenau, the Foreign Minister.

The final threat to Weimar in this period came in November 1923, when there was a putsch in Munich, led by Adolf Hitler. This will be examined on pages 33–35.

▲ **Source E** Soldiers and *Freikorps* troops in Berlin 1920. Note the swastika on some of the helmets and the presence of the flag of the Second Reich, the name given to the German Empire, 1871–1918

ACTIVITIES

1 What grievances did Kapp and the Berlin *Freikorps* have in 1920?
2 Which do think posed the greatest threat to the Weimar Republic, the Spartacists or the Kapp Putsch? Give reasons for your answer.

Practice question

Give two things you can infer from Source E about the *Freikorps*. (*For guidance, see page 78.*)

2.3 The challenges of 1923

The problems facing the Weimar Republic worsened in 1923 due to the French occupation of the Ruhr and the effects of hyperinflation.

Germany had experienced inflation during the First World War and had borrowed extensively to finance its war effort. When the reparations figure was announced – £6,600 million at £100 million per year – the Weimar Government claimed that it could not pay. Moreover, the loss of wealth-making industrial areas exaggerated the problem. As inflation continued, the Weimar Government began to print more money in order to pay in order to pay workers in the Ruhr during the French and Belgian occupation (see below). The value of the German currency started to fall rapidly and, because no reparations were paid, France sent troops into the Ruhr, Germany's main industrial area. The Ruhr is sited in the Rhineland (see Figure 2.1, page 11 and Figure 2.2, page 13) so there were no German troops to stop the French invasion.

The French occupation of the Ruhr, 1923

An occupation by French and Belgium troops took place in January 1923 when Germany again failed to pay reparations to both these countries. The French were angry because they needed the money to help to pay off their own war debts to the USA. The French and Belgians had decided to take the goods they needed, rather than to wait for the Germans to send them.

German resistance

This time the French occupation was met with **passive resistance**. However, the resistance turned sour and Germans carried out acts of industrial sabotage. The German workers in the Ruhr went on strike as a protest against the invasion. Some strikers took more direct action and set factories on fire and sabotaged pumps in some mines so they flooded and could not be worked. A number of strikers were shot by French troops; their funerals led to demonstrations against the invasion. The occupation only served to stir up old enmities and remind people of the war.

The results of the occupation

The invasion certainly united the German people in their hatred of the French and Belgians. The strikers became heroes of the German people as they were standing up to the humiliating Treaty of Versailles and showing that the German people had not been crushed. The German Government backed the strikers and printed more money to pay them a wage. The strike meant that even fewer goods were being produced. The extra strike money plus the collapse in production turned inflation into hyperinflation (see Table 2.2).

Date	Value of mark
July 1914	£1 = 20 marks
Jan 1919	£1 = 35 marks
Jan 1920	£1 = 256 marks
Jan 1921	£1 = 256 marks
Jan 1922	£1 = 764 marks
Jan 1923	£1 = 71,888 marks
July 1923	£1 = 1,413,648 marks
Sept 1923	£1 = 3,954,408,000 marks
Oct 1923	£1 = 1,010,408,000,000 marks
Nov 1923	£1 = 1,680,800,000,000,000 marks

▲ Table 2.2 The decreasing value of the mark against the pound, 1914–23

Hyperinflation

Those people with savings or those on a fixed income found themselves penniless. People were quick to blame the Weimar politicians. This was yet another humiliation for the new government.

Inflation did, however, benefit certain people:

- Businessmen who had borrowed money from the banks were able to pay off these debts.
- Serious food shortages led to a rise in prices of necessities, especially food, which helped farmers.
- Foreigners who were in Germany suddenly found that they had a huge advantage. People who had dollars or pounds found that they could change them for millions of marks and afford things that ordinary Germans could not.

In the summer of 1923, Gustav Stresemann became Chancellor. He began to steady things and introduced a new currency, the Rentenmark. The following year the new currency and loans from the USA (see page 19) enabled an economic recovery. It seemed as if the Weimar Republic had weathered the storms and could look forward to a period of stability and prosperity.

ACTIVITY ?

Why do you think people who had savings in banks suffered more than most in the period of hyperinflation?

Practice questions

1 How useful are Sources F and G for an enquiry into the effects of hyperinflation on Germany? Explain your answer, using Sources F and G and your knowledge of the historical context. (*For guidance, see pages 62–64*.)
2 Explain why there were challenges to the Weimar Republic in the years 1919–23.

You may use the following in your answer:
- The Treaty of Versailles
- The Kapp Putsch

You must also use information of your own.

(*For guidance, see pages 94–95*.)

▲ **Source F** A cartoon published in Germany by the left-wing magazine *Simplicissimus* in 1923. It had the caption 'Paper money' at the top and 'Bread' at the bottom

▲ **Source G** A German woman in 1923, burning currency notes, which burn longer than the amount of firewood they can buy

2.4 What are interpretations of history?

You will have to answer three questions about interpretations in the examination. These are:

1 What is the main difference between these interpretations?
2 Why are these interpretations different?
3 How far do you agree with the view given by one of the interpretations?

An interpretation of history is a view given of the past – an event, a movement, the role of an individual and so on – written at a later date. It could be a view given by an historian, from a textbook, from a history website. The writer has the benefit of hindsight and is able to consult a variety of sources of evidence to give their view of what took place.

There are different interpretations about a past event or person because the writer could focus on or give emphasis to a different aspect of a past event or person, or may have consulted different sources from the past. The writer will carefully choose words and select or omit certain details to emphasise this view. The fact that there are different interpretations of the past does not necessarily mean that one of them is wrong. The two writers might simply have used different sources or they might have used the same sources and reached different conclusions.

Your first task is to identify the view that is given by the interpretation of the event or person. Here is an interpretation of the Treaty of Versailles:

> **Interpretation 1 From** *Versailles and After, 1919–1933* **by Dr Ruth Henig, published in 1995**
>
> Compared to the treaties which Germany had imposed on defeated Russia and Rumania in 1918, the Treaty of Versailles was quite moderate... The Treaty of Versailles was not excessively harsh on Germany, either territorially or economically. However, the German people were expecting victory not defeat. It was the acknowledgement of defeat as much as the treaty terms themselves, which they found so hard to accept.

The view that is given here is:

> This interpretation gives the view that the Treaty of Versailles was not unfair nor too harsh on Germany. It uses phrases such as 'quite moderate' and 'not excessively harsh' to show this view. It also focuses on the harsh treaties that Germany imposed on Russia and Rumania to emphasise the moderate impact of the Treaty on Germany.

Here is a second interpretation of the Treaty of Versailles

> **Interpretation 2 From an online article** *The Treaty of Versailles – the Peace to end all Peace*, **by Alan Woods Monday, 2009**
>
> The Versailles Treaty of 1919 was one of the most outrageous treaties in history. It was a blatant act of plunder perpetrated by a gang of robbers against a helpless, prostrate and bleeding Germany. Among its numerous provisions, it required Germany and its allies to accept full responsibility for causing the war and, under the terms of articles 231–248, to disarm, make substantial territorial concessions and pay reparations to the Entente powers.

And here is an interpretation of the effects of hyperinflation on Germany in 1923:

> **Interpretation 3 From** *Germany 1918–45* **by Richard Radway, published in 1998**
>
> However, not everyone suffered from the effects of hyperinflation in 1923. Many businessmen did well. High inflation could lead to big profits, especially as the increase in wages did not keep pace with the increase in prices. Also many businessmen had borrowed money from the banks and these debts were wiped out. The rise in prices was also good for farmers. In a period of serious inflation food prices will always rise highest. People will give up buying less essential goods before they stop buying food!

ACTIVITY

Read Interpretation 1 and the information underneath it. This outlines the view it gives of the Treaty of Versailles and the evidence it uses. Now try answering the questions below on Interpretations 2 and 3 in a similar way.

Interpretation 2
1 What view does it give of the Treaty of Versailles?
2 What evidence from the interpretation supports this view?
Interpretation 3
3 What view does it give of the effects of hyperinflation in 1923?
4 What evidence from the interpretation supports this view?

You will be given advice in the next three chapters on how to answer interpretation questions.

3 The recovery of the Weimar Republic, 1924–29

Following the crises of 1923, including the French occupation of the Ruhr and hyperinflation, Germany seemed to experience a period of recovery at home and abroad under the direction of Gustav Stresemann and with the assistance of American loans. This, in turn, seemed to encourage greater support for the Weimar Republic and less support for extremist parties such as the Nazis and Communists. However, there are different views about the extent of this recovery. Was Germany too dependent on the USA?

3.1 Reasons for economic recovery

German recovery was largely due to the work of Gustav Stresemann, who was able to work successfully with Britain, France and the USA to improve Germany's economic and international position.

The Dawes Plan

Stresemann realised that Germany could not afford the reparations payments and persuaded the French, British and Americans to change the payment terms through the Dawes Plan, which was agreed in August 1924. It was named after the US vice-president Charles Dawes, who played a leading role in setting up the Plan. The main points of the Plan were:

- Reparation payments would begin at 1 billion marks for the first year and would increase over a period of four years to 2.5 billion marks per year. These payments were far more sensible and manageable and were based upon Germany's capacity to pay.
- The Ruhr area was to be evacuated by Allied occupation troops. This was carried out in 1925.
- The German Reichsbank would be reorganised under Allied supervision.
- The USA would give loans to Germany to help its economic recovery.

The plan was accepted by Germany and the Allies and went into effect in September 1924.

US loans

The Dawes Plan also aimed to boost the German economy through US loans, beginning with a loan of 800 million marks. Over the next six years, USA companies and banks gave loans of nearly US$3,000 million, which not only helped economic recovery, but also enabled Germany to meet the reparations payments.

The Rentenmark

The hyperinflation of 1923 had destroyed the value of the German mark. In November 1923, in order to restore confidence in the German currency, Stresemann introduced a temporary currency called the Rentenmark. This was issued in limited amounts and was based on property values rather than gold reserves. Gradually it restored the confidence of the German people in the currency. In the following year, the Rentenmark was converted into the Reichsmark, a new currency now backed by gold reserves.

The Young Plan

Although Germany was able to meet the reparations payment schedule introduced by the Dawes Plan, the German government regularly complained about the level of payments. In 1929, the Allied Reparations Committee asked US banker Owen Young to investigate and he came up with a new plan for payments. The reparations figure was reduced from £6,600 million to £1,850 million. The length of time Germany had to pay was extended to 59 years with payments at an average of 2.05 billion marks per year.

The Young Plan was a considerable achievement for Stresemann, but it was severely criticised by right-wing politicians such as Alfred Hugenberg and Adolf Hitler, who objected to any further payment of reparations, especially when these were extended to 1988.

Political stability

The period 1924 to 1929 saw greater political stability. Although no single party ever won a majority of seats in the Reichstag, up until 1930 the moderate Social Democrats always won the most votes. Indeed, the period 1924 to 1929 saw greater support for the parties that supported the Weimar Republic, and generally less support for extremist groups such as the Nazis, because of the economic recovery and successes abroad. For example, in May 1924 the Social Democrats had 100 members in the Reichstag, which rose to 153 in May 1928, whereas in May 1924 the Nazis had 32 members, which fell to 12 in May 1928 (see Table 3.1).

This political stability was also due to two key personalities, Stresemann and Paul von Hindenburg. Stresemann's successes abroad made him the most popular political leader of the Weimar Republic. Hindenburg had been one of Germany's war leaders between 1914 and 1918. In 1925, he was elected President, and this seemed to show that the old conservative order now accepted the Republic.

▼ Table 3.1 Election results 1924–28

Party	May 1924	Dec. 1924	May 1928
Social Democrats	100	131	153
National Party (DNVP)	95	103	73
Communist Party (KPD)	62	45	54
Nazi Party (NSDAP)	32	14	12

GUSTAV STRESEMANN 1878–1929

1878 Born in Berlin
1906 Became a Reichstag deputy
1917 Appointed leader of the National Liberal Party (renamed the People's Party in 1919)
1923 Appointed foreign secretary, a post he held until his death in 1929. From August to November, served as Chancellor of Germany and persuaded workers in the Ruhr to call off their passive resistance to the French
1926 Awarded the Nobel Peace Prize for work he had done to improve relations between Germany and France in the 1920s
1929 Died in October, just a few weeks before the Wall Street Crash and the beginning of the Great Depression

Extent of recovery

Compared to the years of inflation and hyperinflation there was recovery, although there are different views about the extent of this recovery.

The German economy seemed to flourish due to the loans from the USA. As a result of hyperinflation, large businesses were able to pay off many of their debts. Industrial growth (see Figure 3.1) was reflected in public works schemes including the building of opera houses and new stadiums.

Many workers were generally better off during this period as wages increased and the average working day remained at eight hours. Moreover, there seemed to be better relations between workers and employers, with fewer strikes between 1924 and 1929. This was the result of state arbitration which, after 1924, took a fairly middle line in disputes, often taking the side of workers.

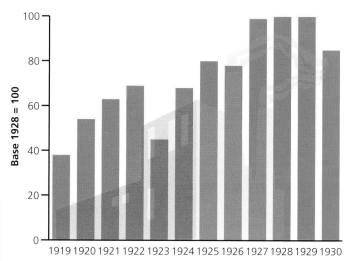

▲ Figure 3.1 Industrial production in Germany, 1919–30

> **Source A** From a German journalist, written in 1930
>
> In comparison with what we expected after Versailles, Germany has raised herself up to shoulder the terrific burden of this peace in a way we would never have thought possible. So that today after ten years we may say with certainty 'Even so, it might have been worse'. The stage of convalescence from Versailles is a very long road to go and we have travelled it surprisingly quickly.

Practice question

Give two things you can infer from Source A about German recovery. *(For guidance, see page 78.)*

Although the Weimar Republic, in the years 1924–29, seemed to recover from the problems of its first five years, the extent of recovery has been questioned, especially the over-dependence on loans from the USA (see Source B).

> **Source B From a speech by Stresemann, 1929**
>
> The economic position is only flourishing on the surface. Germany is in fact dancing on a volcano. If the short-term loans are called in by America, a large section of our economy would collapse.

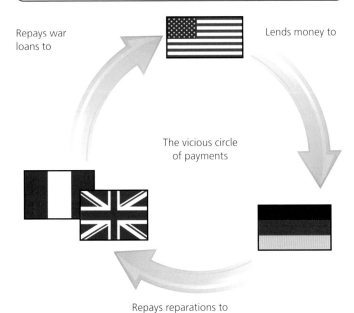

▲ Figure 3.2 The vicious circle of payments

Figure 3.2 shows that the money being borrowed from the USA was in fact being used by Germany to pay reparations to Britain and France. Britain and France then used these payments to repay loans they had received from the USA during the First World War. In addition, as shown in Figure 3.3, unemployment actually increased during this period and reached a peak in 1926.

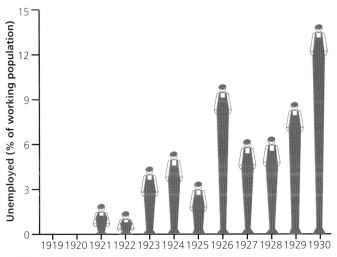

▲ Figure 3.3 Unemployment in Germany, 1919–30

In addition, sections of the German economy were not doing well, especially farmers who experienced problems throughout the 1920s but most especially after 1927. They were affected by a worldwide depression in agriculture and needed to modernise in order to remain competitive both on the home and foreign market. However, lack of profit led them into further debt and discouraged investment in new machinery. In 1929, when industrial production had returned to pre-war levels, agricultural production was still 74 per cent of its pre-war level.

Industrial workers were slightly better off during this period as their wages increased, but their situation had not improved further as their wages did not go much above the rising cost of living.

In addition, the economic recovery did not affect everyone equally. The lower middle class, whose occupations ranged from skilled craftsmen to newer jobs in the civil service, commerce and small businesses, did not fully recover from the hyperinflation of 1923. They felt that their interests were being ignored by the Weimar Republic, which seemed to favour big business.

> **Source C From a history of Germany 1918–45, written in 1997**
>
> However, the German recovery still had serious weaknesses. It depended on American loans which could be withdrawn at any time. Unemployment was a serious problem. The economy might be growing, but it wasn't creating jobs fast enough for Germany's rising population. Some sectors of the economy were in trouble throughout the 1920s, farming in particular.

ACTIVITIES

1 Make a copy of the following table. Organise Sources A, B and C and Figures 3.1, 3.2 and 3.3 into evidence for and against recovery. One has been done for you.

Evidence for recovery	Evidence against recovery
	Source C suggests that Germany is too dependent on the USA

2 Using your table from Activity 1, write a 50-word answer to the question 'To what extent was 1924–29 a period of recovery?'

Practice question

How useful are Sources A and B for an enquiry into German recovery in the years 1924–29? Explain your answer, using Sources A and B and your knowledge of the historical context. (For guidance, see pages 62–64.)

3.2 Stresemann's policies abroad

Stresemann, who was foreign secretary from 1923 to 1929, had several achievements abroad which helped German economic recovery.

The Locarno Pact

Stresemann was determined to improve relations with France and Britain, partly in order to restore Germany's international prestige, but also to gain their co-operation in reducing the worst features of the Treaty of Versailles, especially reparations.

Stresemann realised that France needed to feel secure in order to co-operate over changes in the Versailles peace treaty. Therefore, in 1925 Germany signed the Locarno Pact with Britain, France, Belgium and Italy. By this agreement, the countries agreed to keep existing borders between Germany, Belgium and France. The Locarno Pact marked Germany's return to the European international scene and began a period of co-operation between Germany, France and Britain sometimes described as the 'Locarno honeymoon'.

▲ **Source D** Stresemann signing the Locarno Pact, 1925

The League of Nations

In order for the Locarno Pact to come into operation, Germany had to become a member of the League of Nations, an international organisation established in 1920 to try to maintain peace. In September 1926, Germany was given a permanent seat on the Council of the League of Nations. This confirmed Germany's return to Great Power status and gained considerable prestige for Stresemann. It was a bold move on his part because many Germans regarded the League as the guardian of the hated Treaty of Versailles. Moreover, Stresemann used Germany's position in the League to bring about the Young Plan (see page 19).

The Kellogg–Briand Pact

In 1928 Germany signed the Kellogg–Briand Pact along with 64 other nations. It was agreed that they would keep their armies for self-defence and solve all international disputes 'by peaceful means'. The Pact showed further improved relations between the USA and the leading European nations and fully confirmed that Germany was once again one of these leading nations.

The impact on domestic policies

Stresemann's achievements in foreign policy had an impact on domestic policies and helped the period of recovery.

- Improved relations shown by the Locarno Pact, and Kellogg Briand Pact meant the allies were open to renegotiating the reparations payment schedule. This meant that for the first time the amount of reparation payment was reduced and the timescale for reparation payment was set, making it more manageable and less of a burden economically. However, there was opposition from leading industrialists such as Alfred Hugenberg and Fritz Thyssen who were still against the idea that Germany should have to continue to pay reparations.
- In 1927, Allied troops withdrew from the west bank of the Rhine, five years before scheduled in 1933. This increased morale at home because it showed some relaxation of the terms of the Treaty of Versailles, and boosted the popularity of Stresemann whose policies seemed to be restoring German prestige abroad.

ACTIVITIES ?

1 Source D is a photograph of Stresemann signing the Locarno Pact. Imagine you are the editor of a German newspaper in 1925 that supports Stresemann's policies. Devise a suitable caption for this photograph.

2 Stresemann died in October 1929. Write an obituary for him, focusing on his impact on German recovery.

Practice question

Explain why the Weimar Republic recovered in the years 1924–29.

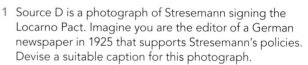

You may use the following in your answer:
- The Dawes Plan
- Achievements abroad

You must also use information of your own.

(For guidance, see pages 94–95.)

3.3 How interpretations differ

This section provides guidance on how to answer the question in the exam that asks how two interpretations differ.

Question

Study Interpretations 1 and 2. They give different views about the extent of German recovery in the years 1924–29. What is the main difference between these views? Explain your answer, using details from both interpretations.

> **Interpretation 1 From *Weimar and Nazi Germany*, F. Reynoldson, published in 1996**
>
> From 1924 to 1929 the Weimar Republic was much stronger than it had been just after the war. Led by Stresemann in the Reichstag, the different parties managed to work together. The extreme parties such as the Nazis gained fewer seats in the elections. The German people were better off and more contented. The Weimar Republic looked safe.

> **Interpretation 2 From *Weimar and Nazi Germany*, E. Wimlott, published in 1997**
>
> German prosperity was built on quicksand foundations. The Weimar economy was dependent upon high-interest American loans, which usually had to be repaid or renewed within three months. In times of depression, US moneylenders could demand rapid repayment. Moreover, unemployment never fell below 1.3 million. Although big business grew in the 1920s, small firms struggled and many went bankrupt.

How to answer

You are being asked to explain the main difference in the views each interpretation has about the German recovery of 1924–29.

Step 1
You will need to identify the main view that Interpretation 1 has about German economic recovery of 1924–29.

Example
Interpretation 1 suggests that the Weimar Republic successfully recovered from the problems it faced after the First World War.

Step 2
You will need evidence from Interpretation 1 to support this view.

Example
I know this because the interpretation suggests that different parties were working together and that there was little support for extreme parties such as the Nazis.

Step 3
You will need to identify the main view that Interpretation 2 has about German economic recovery of 1924–29. Use the phrase 'on the other hand' to show that this interpretation gives a different view.

Example
On the other hand, Interpretation 2 is suggesting that the recovery of the Weimar Republic was built on weak foundations.

Step 4
You will need evidence from Interpretation 2 to support this view.

Example
I know this because the interpretation says that the recovery was too dependent on high-interest American loans.

ACTIVITY

Try explaining the main difference between the different views yourself.

4 Changes in society, 1924–29

The period between 1924 and 1929 is often described as a 'golden age' in the Weimar Republic due to significant changes in culture, the standard of living and the position of women. Indeed, the Weimar period saw an explosion of new cultural ideas in painting, architecture, the theatre and the cinema. Many welcomed these new ideas as they challenged tradition and seemed to strengthen support for the Weimar Republic. Others, however, criticised these changes and believed that they seriously weakened German society and values. For these people, these cultural changes only served to increase their opposition to the Weimar Republic.

4.1 The standard of living

For many Germans, these years saw an improvement in their standard of living, especially in wages, housing and unemployment insurance.

Wages

During this period, German workers did, to a certain extent, benefit from increases in the value of real wages. By 1928 there had been an increase in real wages of over ten per cent which meant Germany had workers some of the best-paid workers in Europe.

However, many of the middle class did not share in this increased prosperity. These changes in real wages were of little benefit to the middle classes, many of who had been bankrupted by the hyperinflation of 1923. They did not really experience a rise in wages and could not claim many of the benefits of the welfare state provided by the Weimar Republic. While unemployment fell generally, it remained high among those who worked in the professions, such as lawyers, civil servants and teachers. In April 1928 almost 184,000 middle-class workers were seeking employment and almost half of them did not qualify for unemployment relief from the state.

Housing

Weimar governments during this period also attempted to deal with a critical shortage of housing in many parts of Germany. They employed architects and planners to devise ways of reducing housing shortages. Government investment, tax breaks, land grants and low-interest loans were used to stimulate the building of new houses and apartments.

Between 1924 and 1931 more than two million new homes were built, while almost 200,000 more were renovated or expanded. By 1929 the state was spending 33 times more on housing than it had been in 1913. By 1928, homelessness had been reduced by more than 60 per cent. The effect of this was to considerably improve the quality of homes for many Germans.

ACTIVITY ?

In what ways did wages, housing and unemployment insurance change in the years 1924–29?

Unemployment insurance

In the 1880s, the German Chancellor, Otto von Bismarck, had introduced a series of reforms which helped the ill and the old, including health, accident and illness insurance schemes. The Weimar Republic extended this with an unemployment insurance law in 1927, which required workers and employees to make contributions to a national scheme for unemployment welfare. Other reforms provided benefits and assistance to war veterans, wives and dependents of the war dead, single mothers and the disabled.

4.2 The position of women

The role of women and debate about their status was an important feature of the Weimar Republic.

Politics

In 1919, women over 20 years old were given the vote and took an increasing interest in politics. The Weimar Constitution also introduced equality in education for the sexes, equal opportunity in civil service appointments and equal pay in the professions. By the end of this period, German women had some of the most advanced legal rights of any country in Europe. Furthermore, by 1926 there were 32 women deputies in the Reichstag, which was a higher proportion than the number in Britain and the USA.

Employment

The proportion of women who took up work outside the home remained much the same during the Weimar Republic.

The most obvious change was in the growing number of women in new areas of employment, most noticeably in public employment, for example the civil service, teaching or social work, in shops or on the assembly line. Furthermore, those who worked in the civil service earned the same as men. By 1933, there were 100,000 women teachers and 3,000 doctors.

This raised the issue of the type of woman who was suitable for such work. Despite the large numbers of women who worked during the war in so called 'men's work', such as heavy industry, after the war the better paid jobs were taken back by men. Married women who worked were often criticised for working and neglecting their homes.

Leisure

Women enjoyed much more freedom socially than had been the case before the Weimar Republic. They went out unescorted, drank and smoked in public, were fashion conscious, often wearing relatively short skirts, had their hair cut short and wore make-up.

▼ Table 4.1 Women in employment in Germany, a comparison between 1907 and 1925. The figures are the percentage of the workforce that was female

Type of employment	1907	1925
Domestic servants	16	11.4
Farm workers	14.5	9.2
Industrial workers	18.3	23
White collar and public employment	6.5	12.6
Percentage of women in employment	31.2	35.6

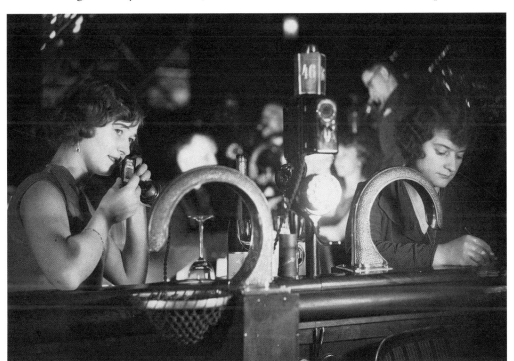

▲ **Source A** German women in a bar, 1930

ACTIVITIES

1 What do you learn from Table 4.1 about employment opportunities for women in Weimar Germany?

2 Using Source A, explain to what extent leisure for women had changed.

4.3 Cultural changes

This period saw the emergence of some of the most exciting art and culture in Europe. The strict pre-war censorship was removed. Throughout the 1920s, Berlin challenged Paris as the cultural capital of Europe, with new and significant developments in painting, cinema, architecture, literature and theatre. However, this led to criticism that artists were undermining traditional German values, especially from right-wing politicians such as Hitler. They said these cultural changes were un-German and immoral.

▼ **Source B** *Grey Day*, 1921, a painting by George Grosz. The man with the moustache is wearing a badge that shows he supports the monarchy rather than the Republic

Art

Before the war most German art had been detached from everyday life. In contrast, most Weimar artists tried to show everyday life. They wanted to be understood by ordinary people and they believed that art should comment on the society of the time. This new approach was given the name *Neue Sachlichkeit*, meaning 'new objectivity', because artists tried to portray society in an objective way. New Objectivity was associated with painters such as George Grosz and Otto Dix.

- George Grosz had served on the front during the First World War and his paintings often show disabled people, along with robot- or doll-like figures who seem to have no control over their lives. His characters are often in depressing cities. He joined the Communist Party in 1918. In 1920, he was taken to court on a charge of insulting the army for the art in one of his exhibitions.
- Otto Dix lived in the cities of Dresden and Berlin during the 1920s. He searched for personalities he could include in paintings to show the uglier side of human nature. He said it was his wartime experiences which had made him aware of this.

Architecture

Architecture also flourished, especially the Bauhaus, which means 'School of Building'. These were architects who designed such various things as chairs, housing estates and cigarette kiosks. Their slogan was 'Art and Technology – a new unity'. Their approach was very different from the elaborate and decorative style of pre-war Germany.

The founder of the Bauhaus movement was Walter Gropius, who believed in using only basic shapes and colours as well as economy in the use of space, materials, time and money. He developed new buildings and furniture using bold designs and unusual materials. When Hitler and the Nazis came to power, Gropius had to leave Germany and eventually settled in America where he became a professor of architecture at Harvard University.

Cinema

This was a golden age for the German cinema with its best-known director Fritz Lang who produced the film *Metropolis*, which is generally acclaimed as the most technically advanced film of the decade.

German actress Marlene Dietrich became one of the most popular films stars in the world and often played strong, mysterious and glamorous women. One of the most popular films, *The Cabinet of Dr Caligari*, was a horror film but its underlying message was anti-war and anti-military.

Literature

This period encouraged literature from both the right and left in politics.

- On the political right, writers such as Arthur Moeller and Oswald Spengler were highly critical of German democracy and glorified the experiences of the First World War.
- On the left, writers such as Erich Remarque and Ludwig Renn were very anti-war. Remarque wrote a moving anti-war novel called *All Quiet on the Western Front* (Source C) which describes the horrors of the First World War and, within three months, was turned into a very successful film.

> **Source C** From *All Quiet on the Western Front* by Erich Remarque, published in 1929
>
> Our faces are encrusted, our thoughts are devastated, we are weary to death; when the attack comes we shall have to strike many of the men with our fists to waken them and make them come with us – our eyes are burnt, our hands are torn, our knees bleed, our elbows are raw. How long has it been? Weeks – months – years? Only days. We see time pass in the colourless faces of the dying.

Theatre

Another important cultural change was the emergence of new operas and plays. These were called *Zeittheater* and *Zeitoper*, which means theatre and opera 'of the time' and featured greater realism. For example, the heroine of one opera sings in a bathtub! In Erwin Piscator's *The Salesman of Berlin* three street-sweepers sweep away the worst features of the years after 1918, including a pile of paper money, a steel helmet, which represents Germany's defeated army, and the body of the man who had worn it. In Piscator's adaptation of Jaroslav Hašek's novel *The Good Soldier Schweik,* the hero delivers his criticisms of Germany as he sits in the toilet.

ACTIVITIES

1 What new ideas influenced cultural change in Germany during the years 1924–29, especially in art and architecture?

2 What can you learn from Source B about attitudes to the Weimar Republic?

3 What image is given by Source C about the First World War?

4 The period 1924–29 is often described as a 'golden age' in the Weimar Republic. Working in pairs, copy and complete the following table using pages 24–7. One of you should complete evidence for and the other against, and then compare your findings. Then have a go at the practice question below.

	Evidence for golden age	Evidence against
Wages		
Housing		
Unemployment		
Women		
Culture		

Practice question

Explain why 1924–29 was a golden age in the Weimar Republic.

You may use the following in your answer:
- Women
- Culture

You must also use information of your own.

(For guidance, see pages 94–95.)

KEY TOPIC 2

Hitler's rise to power, 1919–33

This key topic examines the rise to power of Hitler and the Nazi Party, from the setting up of the Nazi Party in 1920 to how Hitler became Chancellor in January 1933. It explains the early features of the Nazi Party including the establishment of the Sturmabteilung (SA), the key features and consequences of Hitler's failed attempt to seize power in Munich in 1923, and how Hitler reorganised the Nazi Party in the years 1925–28 in preparation for it to achieve power through legal methods.

Each chapter within this key topic explains a key issue and examines important lines of enquiry as outlined in the boxes below. There will also be further guidance on how to answer the interpretations question:

- ■ How to answer the second question on interpretations, suggesting one reason why they give different views. (pages 37–38)
- ■ How to answer the third question on interpretations: how far do you agree with one of the interpretations? (page 51)

CHAPTER 5 THE DEVELOPMENT OF THE NAZI PARTY, 1920–29

- ■ Hitler's early career: joining the German Workers' Party and setting up the Nazi Party, 1919–20.
- ■ The early growth and features of the Party. The Twenty-Five Point Programme. The role of the SA.
- ■ The reasons for, events and consequences of the Munich Putsch.
- ■ The reasons for limited support for the Nazi Party in the years 1924–28. Party reorganisation and *Mein Kampf*. The Bamberg Conference of 1926.

CHAPTER 6 THE GROWTH IN SUPPORT FOR THE NAZIS, 1929–33

- ■ The growth of unemployment, its causes and impacts. The failure of successive Weimar governments to deal with unemployment from 1929 to January 1933. The growth of support for the Communist Party.
- ■ The reasons for the growth of support for the Nazi Party, including the appeal of Hitler and the Nazis, the effect of propaganda and the work of the SA.
- ■ Political developments in 1932. The roles of Hindenburg, Brüning, Papen and Schleicher.
- ■ The parts played by Hindenburg and Papen in Hitler becoming Chancellor in 1933.

TIMELINE

1919	Hitler joins the German Workers' Party	1929	Death of Stresemann, Wall Street Crash
1920	Hitler sets up the Nazi Party	1930	Nazis win 107 seats in Reichstag
1921	Hitler introduces the SA	1932 July	Nazis win 230 seats in Reichstag, Papen becomes Chancellor
1923	The Munich Putsch		
1925	*Mein Kampf* published	1932 November	Nazis win 196 seats in Reichstag Schleicher becomes Chancellor
1926	Bamberg Conference		
1928	Nazis win 12 seats in Reichstag	1933 January	Hitler becomes Chancellor

5 The development of the Nazi Party, 1920–29

When the First World War ended, Germany experienced tremendous social and political upheaval. During the five years after the war, several new parties emerged and there were communist and right-wing uprisings. One of the new parties was the DAP (*Deutsche Arbeiterpartei*). As it grew, it added the words 'national' and 'socialist' to become the NSDAP and during its transformation it acquired a new leader, Adolf Hitler. Hitler changed the DAP from a small number of malcontents to a party which tried to take over the Bavarian state government in 1923. The attempted takeover failed, but by the end of 1923 Hitler had gained considerable publicity. Hitler became well known not only in Germany but also across Europe and in the years 1925–28 he did much to reorganise the Nazi Party.

5.1 Hitler's early career

Hitler's early life and career did not suggest that he would eventually achieve such prominence.

Adolf Hitler was born in the village of Braunau am Inn, Austria-Hungary in 1889. Not especially successful at school, Hitler was shaped by three events as he grew up. His father died in 1903 and the death brought Adolf much closer to his mother. He frequently said that he had never been close to his father and it is thought that they disagreed about Adolf's future choice of career. Adolf wanted to attend art college and his father wanted him to work in the civil service. The death of his mother in 1907 was the second important event. On his mother's death, the family doctor said, 'I have never seen anyone so prostrate with grief as Adolf Hitler.'

▲ Figure 5.1 Adolf Hitler, aged ten in 1899

That same year saw the third event. Hitler's application to the Academy of Fine Arts Vienna was rejected, as was a further one the following year. For the next five years (1908–13) he spent an odd existence spending the money he inherited and then living rough, earning a living by selling his own hand-painted postcards.

Hitler fled to Munich in Germany in 1913 to avoid military service in the Austrian army. On the outbreak of war, while in Munich, he volunteered to join the German army, feeling that this now provided him with a purpose in life. Because he was not a German citizen, a special dispensation had to be provided to allow him to join up. Hitler served in the 16th Bavarian Reserve Infantry Regiment and saw action on the Western Front, including the Battle of the Somme. He was a brave soldier and won the Iron Cross Second Class in 1914 and First Class in 1918. He reached the rank of *Gefreite* – lance corporal. At the end of the war, Hitler was in hospital, temporarily blinded by a gas attack. He was angered by Germany's surrender. He blamed the politicians for surrendering, and accepted the idea of the *Dolchstoss* (see page 12).

> **Source A** From *Mein Kampf*, written by Hitler in 1924. Here he is describing his time in Vienna
>
> My life was a continuous struggle with hunger ... I had but one pleasure – my books. At that time I read enormously and thoroughly ... In this way I forged in a few years' time the foundation of a knowledge from which I still draw nourishment today ... In this period there took shape within me a world picture and a philosophy which became the granite foundation of all my acts. In addition to what I then created, I have had to learn little and I have had to alter nothing.

Practice question

Give two things you can infer from Source A about Hitler's early career. *(For guidance, see page 78.)*

ACTIVITY

Create a timeline for Hitler's life from birth to 1919.

5.2 The early growth of the Nazi Party

As in most of Germany at the end of the war, there was political chaos in the state of Bavaria and its capital, Munich. During 1919, the Communists had seized power in Munich but, on the orders of Ebert, the *Freikorps* quickly removed them (see page 14). At the beginning of 1919, in the atmosphere of political chaos, Anton Drexler founded the German Workers' Party (*Deutsche Arbeiterpartei, DAP*). The party was right wing and was one of many founded in Bavaria at this time. Drexler and his followers were quite socialist in some of their ideas – restricting the profits of companies, wanting a classless society – but the party was also very nationalistic. The DAP also stressed the *völkisch* idea – the notion of a pure German people. By the summer of 1919, the DAP remained small, with about fifty members, but it attracted the attention of the political department of the army, which was on the lookout for any organisation that might be indoctrinating the people in socialist ways.

Hitler and the German Workers' Party

At the end of the First World War, Hitler was angry about the defeat of Germany and hated the new Weimar Republic. He remained in the army and became an informant with its intelligence department in Munich. In September 1919, one of his duties was to attend and report on a meeting of the German Workers' Party (DAP). At the meeting, Hitler was angered by the comments one of the speakers made and he made a powerful speech in reply. Drexler was so impressed by Hitler that he asked him to join the party, and according to Hitler in *Mein Kampf* (Hitler's autobiography) he joined shortly afterwards. However, recent historical research has shown that Hitler was encouraged by his army superiors to join the party. Nevertheless, joining the party started Hitler on a political journey which saw him become the leader of Germany within fourteen years.

▼ **Source B** Photograph of Hitler, on the right, with two fellow soldiers and his dog, Foxl, 1915. He remained in the army after the end of the war.

In the DAP, Hitler discovered that he was good at public speaking. His enthusiasm was soon rewarded within the party when he was made responsible for recruitment and propaganda. He spoke at several meetings and his standard themes were·

- the *Dolchstoss*
- his disgust at the Treaty of Versailles
- his hatred of Weimar and the November Criminals
- what he saw as the communist–Jewish conspiracy bent on destroying Germany.

Source C From a letter written by Hitler in 1921

During the Communist attempt to take over in Munich, I remained in the army ... In my talks as an education officer, I attacked the bloodthirsty Red dictatorship ... In 1919, I joined the German Workers' Party, which then had seven members, and I believed that I had found a political movement in keeping with my own ideas.

ACTIVITIES ?

1 What were the main ideas of the DAP?

2 What does Source C show about Hitler's political ideas in 1919?

3 Copy the themes of Hitler's speeches then add two or three sentences explaining why Hitler chose to speak about each one.

The NSDAP, 1920–23

In February 1920, Hitler and Drexler wrote what became known as the Twenty-Five Point Programme (Table 5.1). It was a political manifesto and Hitler kept to most of the ideas throughout the rest of his life. The programme was announced at a key meeting in Munich and shortly after 'national socialist' was added to the party's name. The party grew rapidly in 1920 and Hitler was largely responsible for this – his public speaking attracted hundreds to meetings of the NSDAP. (The word 'Nazi' comes from *Nationalsozialistische*. The Social Democratic Party (SPD) were called the 'Sozis'.)

Increased membership meant the party was able to buy up and publish its own newspaper – the *Völkischer Beobachter* (*People's Observer*). Hitler's influence on the party was such that he became its leader in July 1921, and began to develop his ideas on how he should lead the party. He had the title Führer (leader) but he gradually developed the word to have a much more powerful meaning. For him, it meant that he had to have absolute power and authority in the party and that he was answerable to no one. This was the *Führerprinzip* (the leadership principle) and came to be a cornerstone of the party organisation.

▼ Table 5.1 Key points of the Twenty-Five Point Programme

Point	Content
1	The union of all Germans to form a Greater Germany.
2	The scrapping of the Treaty of Versailles.
4	Citizenship of the state to be granted only to people of German blood. Therefore, no Jew was to be a citizen of the nation.
6	The right to vote in elections to be allowed only to German citizens.
7	Foreign nationals to be deported if it became impossible to feed the entire population.
8	All non-Germans who entered the country after 1914 to leave.
13	The government to nationalise all businesses that had been formed into corporations.
14	The government to profit-share in major industries.
17	An end to all speculation in land and any land needed for communal purposes to be seized. There would be no compensation.
23	All newspaper editors and contributors to be German, and non-German papers to appear only with the permission of the government.
24	Religious freedom for all – providing the views expressed did not threaten or offend the German people.
25	The creation of a strong central government for the Reich to put the new programme into effect.

ACTIVITIES

1 Explain what is meant by the *Führerprinzip*.
2 Study the Twenty-Five Point Programme shown in Table 5.1. Copy the table below and insert which parts of the programme relate to each particular area.

Treaty of Versailles	Race	Religion	Civil rights	Industry

3 Find out what the other points in the Twenty-Five Point Programme were and add them to your table.
4 Work in pairs. What does the Twenty-Five Point Programme show you about the ideology of the early Nazi Party?

The role of the *Sturmabteilung*

As leader of the Nazi Party, Hitler began to make some changes. He adopted the swastika (*Hakenkreuz* – hook-cross) as the emblem of the party and the use of the raised arm salute.

The political meetings in Munich at this time generated much violence and, in order to protect Nazi speakers, protection squads were used. These men were organised into the Gymnastic and Sports Section, which was developed into the SA (*Sturmabteilung*), in 1921, led by Ernst Röhm. The members of the SA were more commonly known as the 'Brownshirts' because of the colour of their uniform. The SA became the private army of the Nazi Party and pledged loyalty and obedience to it (see Source D). During the period 1921–23, the SA was used to disrupt the meetings of the Social Democratic Party and the Communist Party.

> **Source D** The pledge of loyalty and obedience taken by members of the SA
>
> As a member of the NSDAP, I pledge myself by its storm flag to:
>
> ■ be always ready to stake life and limb in the struggle for the aims of the movement
> ■ give absolute military obedience to my military superiors and leaders
> ■ bear myself honourably in and out of service.

Hitler ensured that there was maximum publicity for his party and membership grew from about 1,100 in June 1920 to about 55,000 in November 1923. His speeches had the usual anti-Weimar criticisms, but also contained growing references to the purity of the German (or Aryan) race and vitriolic comments about Jews. For Hitler and his followers, the Jews were becoming the scapegoat for all Germany's problems. Although at this point the Nazi Party was essentially a regional organisation with its main support in Bavaria (see Figure 5.2), this did not stop Hitler having national political aims.

Source E A member of the Nazi Party describing one of Hitler's speeches in 1922

My critical faculty was swept away. Leaning forward as if he were trying to force his inner self into the consciousness of all these thousands, he was holding the masses, and me with them, under a hypnotic spell by the sheer force of his belief ... I forgot everything but the man; then glancing around, I saw that his magnetism was holding these thousands as one.

◀ Figure 5.2 Map showing Germany and Bavaria

ACTIVITIES

1 What can you learn about the SA (*Sturmabteilung*) from Source D?

2 Study Source E. According to this source, what made Hitler a good speaker?

Practice question

How useful are Sources D and E for an enquiry into the early Nazi Party? Explain your answer, using Sources D and E and your knowledge of the historical context.
(*For guidance, see pages 62–64.*)

5.3 The Munich Putsch

When the economic and political crises of 1923 hit Germany, Hitler decided that the Nazi Party was in a position to overthrow the regional government in Munich and could then march on Berlin. Hitler detested the Weimar Republic and, following the invasion of the Ruhr by the French and the onset of hyperinflation (see page 17), he felt that Weimar was now so disgraced it could easily be toppled. The Nazi Party had grown in strength and popularity in Munich and Bavaria. Therefore, he decided his first step would be to seize control of Bavaria and then Berlin. He would then remove the weak Weimar politicians and form his own Nazi government. Figure 5.3 summarises the reasons why Hitler launched the Munich Putsch.

As membership of the Nazi Party grew and as he became a well-known figure in Bavarian politics, Hitler began to consider the idea of launching himself on to the national scene. He had been impressed by Benito Mussolini's seizure of power in Italy in 1922. Mussolini, leader of the Italian National Fascist Party, had used his private army (the Blackshirts) to seize power after marching on the capital. Hitler saw that Mussolini had the support of the regular army and knew that he would have to win over the *Reichswehr* (German army and navy) if a march on Berlin took place. The government of Bavaria, headed by Gustav von Kahr, along with the army chief Otto von Lossow and police chief Hans Seisser, had never fully supported Weimar. Hitler knew that if he could win the support of these three important men then an attack on the Weimar government in Berlin was feasible.

▼ Figure 5.3 Reasons for the Munich Putsch. The photo shows town Councillors from the left being arrested on 8 November 1923

German humiliation following the French occupation of the Ruhr. Many Germany people were furious that the Weimar Republic eventually called off passive resistance to the French occupation

Hitler detested Versailles and wanted to remove the terms of the treaty

Hitler had won the support of General Ludendorff, the former army Commander-in-Chief, an extremely popular figure

Hitler hated the Weimar Republic

The SA would be used as armed support

Weimar was disgraced; Hitler believed people across Germany would support him instead

Hitler was confident that Kahr and the army in Bavaria would support him

Growth of the Nazi Party. The Nazi party had increase support by 1923, especially in Bavaria

Weimar blamed for hyperinflation

ACTIVITIES

1 Why was it important for Hitler to have the support of the *Reichswehr* if he attacked Berlin?
2 Study the diagram of the reasons for the Munich Putsch (Figure 5.3). Work in pairs to decide the rank order of importance of the reasons. Explain why you have ranked them this way.
3 Why did Hitler think he would win national support in his bid to seize power in Germany in 1923?

Practice question

Explain why Hitler carried out the Munich Putsch.

You may use the following in your answer:
- Ludendorff
- French occupation of the Ruhr

You must also use information of your own.

(For guidance, see pages 94–95.)

Source F Hitler's announcement at the beginning of the Munich Putsch on 9 November 1923

Proclamation to the German people! The Government of the November Criminals in Berlin has today been deposed. A provisional German National Government has been formed, which consists of General Ludendorff, Adolf Hitler and Colonel von Seisser.

Key features of the Munich Putsch

On the evening of 8 November 1923, Hitler and 600 Nazis seized the Bürgerbräukeller (a huge beer hall in Munich), where Kahr, Seisser and Lossow were attending a political meeting. Hitler placed the three leaders in a room and won promises of support for his planned takeover from them after they had been held at gunpoint. This event is known as the Munich Putsch. Remarkably, the three leaders were allowed to leave the building, and the following day Seisser and Lossow changed their minds and organised troops and police to resist Hitler's planned armed march through Munich.

Despite his plans having fallen apart, Hitler continued with the march through Munich. However, the Nazis had only about 2,000 rifles and when they were challenged they were no match for the well-armed police force. As the two opposing forces met, shots were fired and 16 Nazis and four police officers were killed. The incident was soon over and the Nazis scattered. Hitler disappeared but was arrested two days later on the day that the Nazi Party was banned.

▲ **Source G** Armed SA men at a barricade in Munich, 9 November 1923. The future leader of the SS, Heinrich Himmler, is holding the Second Reich flag (pre-1918) in the middle of the photograph

ACTIVITIES

1 Study Source F. Can you suggest reasons why some Germans might have supported Hitler in the Putsch?

2 What can you learn from Source G about the SA in 1923?

3 Using a mind map, summarise the main reasons for the failure of the Putsch.

The importance of the Munich Putsch

Hitler was arrested along with his main supporter, Erich Ludendorff, and was tried for treason. The trial began in February 1924 and lasted almost one month. The trial gave Hitler nationwide publicity and introduced him to the German public via the national press. He denied the charge of treason. Hitler insisted that he was simply attempting to restore Germany's greatness and was resisting the weak and feeble Weimar government. He poured scorn on the November Criminals, the Treaty of Versailles and 'those Jewish Bolshevists' who had betrayed Germany. Hitler believed that they had betrayed Germany by agreeing to the armistice in 1918 and, in the following year, signing the Treaty of Versailles. He attacked Weimar at every available opportunity and used the trial to put forward his political views. The sympathetic judges allowed him to make long speeches, which were then reported in national newspapers. As a result, Hitler became famous in Germany.

Hitler was found guilty of treason but the judges treated him leniently. Ludendorff was not charged.

On 1 April, Hitler was sentenced to five years, the minimum sentence to be served in Landsberg Prison. He served only nine months, and while there, he completed his autobiography *Mein Kampf* (*My Struggle*), which also contained his political views (see Figure 5.4). The sentence allowed him time to reflect on the Putsch and his future in politics (see Source H). Historians now believe that it was in Landsberg that Hitler came to the conclusion that he was the leader needed to make Germany great again. He had a relatively easy time in gaol and he was permitted as many visitors as he wanted. He received large amounts of mail and was able to access whatever books he wanted.

The impact of the Putsch on the Nazi Party

The immediate consequences of the Putsch were Hitler's imprisonment and the Nazi Party going into decline. However, in the longer term Hitler and the Nazi Party gained from the failed Putsch:

- Hitler's trial was a propaganda success for the Nazi Party – Hitler made himself known nationally and won support from other nationalists.
- Hitler realised that he needed to have complete control over the Party to guarantee its future success.
- Hitler realised that coups did not work and that the Nazi Party would need to use legal means to gain power – by winning elections.

This all meant that the development of the Party changed from 1924 onwards (see page 36).

> **Source H** Comments made by Hitler as a prisoner in Landsberg. He was speaking to a fellow Nazi inmate
>
> When I resume active work, it will be necessary to follow a new policy. Instead of working to achieve power by armed conspiracy, we shall have to hold our noses and enter parliament against the Catholic and Communist members. If out-voting them takes longer than out-shooting them, at least the results will be guaranteed by their own constitution. Sooner or later, we shall have a majority in parliament.

ACTIVITIES

1 Using a flow diagram, summarise the causes, events and results of the Munich Putsch.

2 Working in pairs, compare the key ideas in *Mein Kampf* to the Twenty-Five Point Programme (see page 31). What similarities are there between them?

Practice question

Give two things you can infer from Source H about Hitler's views on politics. (*For guidance, see page 78.*)

- Abolition of the Treaty of Versailles
- Gain *Lebensraum* (living space) to create a greater Germany where all German-speaking people would be incorporated into the nation
- Key ideas of *Mein Kampf*
- Creation of a *Volksgemeinschaft* (people's community) – the strongest races would dominate the weakest in Germany
- All ills in German society were caused by Jews. All Jews to be eliminated from Germany

▲ Figure 5.4 The key ideas of *Mein Kampf*

5.4 The lean years, 1924–28

In the period 1924–28 the Nazi Party lost support but was reorganised by Hitler.

Reorganisation of the Nazi Party

The fortunes of the party declined when Hitler was in prison. It had been banned but survived secretly. The replacement leader, Alfred Rosenberg, had few leadership qualities and the party split into rival groups. On his release from prison, Hitler persuaded the President of Bavaria to lift the ban on the Nazi Party. In February, the Nazi Party was re-launched and Hitler began to take control once again. This meant making changes to the party and its structure. It was decided to create party branches, called *Gaue* (single *Gau*), each led by a *Gauleiter*. Hitler made sure that only his closest associates helped run the party from Munich, and these people and the *Gauleiter* pushed the idea of the *Führerprinzip* (see page 31).

At the Bamberg party conference in 1926, Hitler continued to strengthen his position as leader of the party. Possible rivals to Hitler's leadership, such as Gregor Strasser and Josef Goebbels, were won over. Strasser was appointed propaganda leader for the party and Goebbels was made *Gauleiter* of Berlin. Other opponents were removed. For example, Hitler forced Ernst Röhm (see page 32) to resign as leader of the SA because he was concerned that the SA would continue to be a violent group. He could not guarantee that Röhm would follow his orders. The new leader of the SA was Franz Pfeffer von Salomon. Hitler then created his own bodyguard, the *Schutzstaffel* (SS). He also set up the *Hitlerjugend* (Hitler Youth) to rival other youth groups.

By 1926, Hitler was now the undisputed leader – *der Führer* – and his message was to use endless propaganda to win over the voters. The Twenty-Five Point Programme of 1920 was accepted as the cornerstone of Nazi Party policy. However, in 1928, Point 17 (see page 31) was amended to

say that privately owned land would only be confiscated if it was owned by a Jew. Before 1928, Hitler had tried to win the support of urban voters, but now he decided that rural voters should be targeted. This came at the time when farmers began to experience economic problems and to find Nazism attractive.

Progress?

Hitler's leadership and reorganisation of the party achieved results. The party had only 27,000 members in 1925 but exceeded 100,000 by the end of 1928. It was a nationwide party that had begun to attract all classes. Yet, despite the changes, the Nazis won only 12 seats in parliament in the 1928 elections, having held 32 in 1924. There were further changes within the Nazi Party in the late 1920s when Hitler began to target the peasants as a key electoral group. He also replaced Strasser as head of party propaganda with Josef Goebbels.

The political and economic events of 1929 (see pages 39–40) helped the Nazi Party rise from relative obscurity to become one of the leading parties in the country. The 'lean years' were at an end.

ACTIVITIES ?

1 Why do you think Point 17 of the Twenty-Five Point Programme was altered?

2 Create an election poster for the Nazi Party for 1928, showing that it has changed since the Munich Putsch.

3 Working in pairs, make a copy of and complete the following table about the progress made by the Nazi Party in the years 1920–29. One of you complete the section on progress and the other on the lack of progress.

	Progress	Lack of progress
1920–22		
Munich Putsch		
1924–29		

Practice question

How useful are Sources H (page 35) and I for an enquiry into the development of the Nazi Party, 1924–29? Explain your answer, using Sources H and I and your knowledge of the historical context. (*For guidance, see pages 62–64.*)

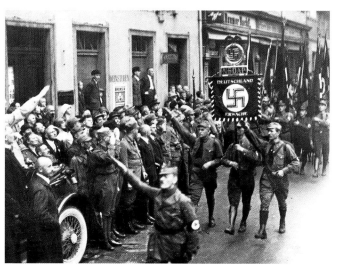

◀ **Source I** Hitler at a Nazi Party rally, Weimar, July 1926. Hitler is standing in the car on the left of the photo with his arm raised

5.5 Why the interpretations differ

This section provides guidance on how to answer the question which asks you to suggest one reason why the interpretations give different views. Look at the question below. Then read the guidance on how to answer it on page 38.

Question

Suggest one reason why Interpretations 1 and 2 give different views about the extent of German recovery in the years 1924–29. You may use the Sources A and B to help explain your answer.

Interpretation 1 From *Weimar and Nazi Germany*, F. Reynoldson, published in 1996

From 1924 to 1929 the Weimar Republic was much stronger than it had been just after the war. Led by Stresemann in the Reichstag, the different parties managed to work together. The extreme parties such as the Nazis gained fewer seats in the elections. The German people were better off and more contented. The Weimar Republic looked safe.

Interpretation 2 From *Weimar and Nazi Germany*, E. Wimlott, published in 1997

German prosperity was built on quicksand foundations. The Weimar economy was dependent upon high-interest American loans, which usually had to be repaid or renewed within three months. In times of depression, US money lenders could demand rapid repayment. Moreover, unemployment never fell below 1.3 million. Although big business grew in the 1920s, small firms struggled and many went bankrupt.

Source A From a speech by Stresemann, 1929

The economic position is only flourishing on the surface. Germany is in fact dancing on a volcano. If the short-term loans are called in by America, a large section of our economy would collapse.

Source B From a German journalist, written in 1930

In comparison with what we expected after Versailles, Germany has raised herself up to shoulder the terrific burden of this peace in a way we would never have thought possible. So that today after ten years we may say with certainty 'Even so, it might have been worse'. The stage of convalescence from Versailles is a very long road to go and we have travelled it surprisingly quickly.

How to answer

On page 23 you were shown how to explain one difference between these two interpretations. Now you have to give one reason why these interpretations are different. You can use the sources to help you with this answer.

There are three reasons as to why the two interpretations differ. You will only need to give one of these.

First possible reason (remember you only have to explain one of the reasons)

The interpretations may differ because they have given weight to two different sources. You need to identify the views given in the two sources.

Source B suggests that the recovery was too dependent on the USA and could soon collapse. Source A suggests that the recovery was very successful after the problems caused by the Treaty of Versailles.

Now you need to show how the sources match the views of the two interpretations and identify the views given in the interpretations that match.

Source B provides some support for Interpretation 2, which stresses that the recovery of the Republic was based on weak foundations. Source A provides some support for Interpretation 1 which suggests that the Republic recovered well from the problems it had faced after the First World War.

Second possible reason (remember you only have to explain one of the reasons)

The interpretations may differ because they are partial extracts and in this case they do not actually contradict one another. Remember to make reference to the views given in each interpretation.

Both interpretations suggest that the Weimar Republic did recover in the years 1924-29. Interpretation 1 says that there was political recovery and Interpretation 2 emphasises the economic recovery, which was dependent on American loans.

Third possible reason (remember you only have to explain one of the reasons)

They may differ because the authors have a different emphasis.

Interpretation 1 focuses more on the political recovery of the Republic especially compared to the years after the First World War. On the other hand, Interpretation 2 focuses more on the economic recovery and the over-dependence on the USA.

6 The growth in support for the Nazis, 1929–33

As you saw in Chapter 3, Germany was able to recover under Stresemann. Nevertheless, there were some who were experiencing problems by 1928, namely farmers. The Wall Street Crash in October 1929 led to a depression in the USA, which then spread around the world. US loans to Germany were called in and unemployment began to rise as companies collapsed. By 1932, there were about 6 million unemployed. The economic problems led to political discontent and extreme parties were able to secure support in the elections. In the period 1929–33, the Nazis became the largest political party in Germany. Hitler was able to appeal to all classes of society; his simple messages and slogans could be understood by all. The Depression suited the Nazi Party and by January 1933, Hitler had become the Chancellor of Germany.

6.1 Unemployment and its impact

By 1929, much of Germany had experienced five years of prosperity. The loans from the USA had helped to remove inflation and there had been much investment in industry. However, the prosperity depended on the USA. When its stock market collapsed in October 1929 – the Wall Street Crash – the problems created had huge consequences for the German economy. The death of Stresemann also added to the crisis. It was felt that he was the only person who would be able to steer Germany through troubled times again.

Bankers and financiers in the USA now recalled the loans made to Germany in 1924 under the Dawes Plan. International trade began to contract and German exports fell rapidly in the years after 1929. The Great Depression had arrived in Germany. Unemployment began to rise as employers sacked workers and factories closed. German farmers had already been experiencing problems and the continued fall in food prices worsened their plight.

Some Germans were unable to pay their rents and found themselves living on the streets (see Source A).

Successive Weimar governments, more especially the Brüning government of 1930–32, failed to deal with the problem of unemployment, although some measures were tried there was little agreement on the best way to reduce it.

- The Müller government (1928–30) was in power when Germany was first affected by the Depression. The members of the government were split over whether to increase unemployment contributions from 3 to 3.5 per cent to pay for the increased numbers out of work and. In March 1930, Müller resigned.
- The new Chancellor, Brüning, believed that the best way to deal with the depression and unemployment was to balance the budget by reducing spending and raising taxes. In March 1930, he introduced a wage cut of 2.5 per cent for civil servants. This was blocked by the SDP in the Reichstag. President Hindenburg backed his Chancellor and used Article 48 of the Constitution (see page 9) to decree the wage cut.
- He increased the tax rates on things such as income, beer and sugar and introduced some new taxes.
- He made further cuts to the pay of civil servants so that by the end of 1931 their pay had been reduced by 23 per cent. Brüning also made very unpopular cuts of up to 60 per cent to unemployment benefit.

These harsh remedies made the crisis deeper and more businesses continued to fail. Brüning was given the nickname of the 'Hunger Chancellor'. The unemployed and hungry

> **Source A** From 'A fairytale of Christmas', a short story written in 1931 by Rudolf Leonhard, a member of the Communist Party (KPD). Leonhard was writing about the unemployed in Germany
>
> No one knew how many of them there were. They completely filled the streets ... They stood or lay about in the streets as if they had taken root there. The streets were grey, their faces were grey, and even the hair on their heads and the stubble on the cheeks of the youngest there was grey with dust and their adversity.

> **Practice question**
>
> Give two things you can infer from Source A about the effects of unemployment. (*For guidance, see page 78.*)

wanted solutions that the Weimar governments couldn't offer, and looked to other political parties to relieve their suffering.

Unemployment continued to rise in the early 1930s and by January 1932 the total unemployed exceeded 6 million (see Figure 6.2 on page 40). This meant that four out of every ten German workers were without jobs. Unlike 1923, the fear in Germany this time was not inflation, it was unemployment. If a political party could offer clear and simple solutions to the economic problems, it would readily win votes. The workers wanted jobs and the middle classes feared a Communist revolution like the one that had occurred in Russia in 1917. The German Communist Party (KPD) was growing and promised a way out of the depression.

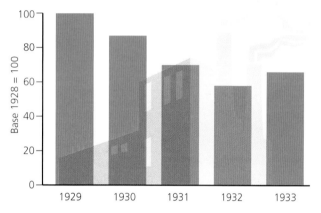

▲ Figure 6.1 German industrial production, 1929–33

▼ **Source B** Unemployed in Hanover, queuing for their benefits in 1932. Note the writing on the wall of the building. Translated it says 'Vote Hitler'

ACTIVITIES ?

1. Study Figure 6.1 and Figure 6.2. What can you learn from these charts about the impact of the Great Depression on Germany in the years to 1933?

2. In what ways is Source B helpful in understanding the situation in Germany in 1932?

3. Construct a mind map to show the effects of the Great Depression on Germany.

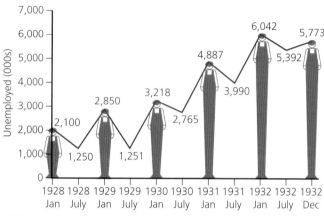

▲ Figure 6.2 Unemployment in Germany, 1928–32

Practice question

How useful are Sources A (on page 39) and B for an enquiry into the effects of unemployment on Germany? Explain your answer, using Sources A and B and your knowledge of the historical context. *(For guidance, see pages 62–64.)*

Impact on the Weimar government

The economic crisis created problems for the Weimar government and there was little agreement about how to tackle unemployment and poverty. In March 1930, Heinrich Brüning of the Centre Party succeeded Müller as Chancellor, and because he did not have a majority he relied on President Hindenburg and Article 48. After this, the Reichstag was used less frequently. Historians see this as the death of Weimar.

Brüning called a general election in September 1930 in the hope of winning a majority in the Reichstag. The Nazis made a breakthrough, winning 107 seats, and were the second largest party after the Social Democrats which won 143. Brüning's lack of a majority forced him to rely more and more on President Hindenburg (see Table 6.1).

Brüning's reduction of government spending only served to lose him support of the unemployed and led to him being nicknamed the 'hunger Chancellor'. The people of Germany were extremely tired of shortages of food – and were now experiencing shortages for the third time in sixteen years. When some German banks collapsed in the financial crisis of 1931, foreign investors withdrew their assets and hopes of recovery were hit further. The one encouraging effect of the economic crisis was the suspension of reparations payments in 1931. Nevertheless, the economic situation remained bleak.

Brüning resigned in May 1932 and during his time as Chancellor the right-wing Nazi Party had had successes in the regional and general elections.

Moreover, during the next eight months there was continued political and economic turmoil which saw the extreme parties become more violent. Some of the changes brought in by Brüning had made some improvements, but it was too little too late. The Depression seemed to have unleashed chaos across Germany, which resulted in Hitler gaining more and more support and becoming Chancellor in January 1933 (see page 49).

The German Communist party

One of the reasons for increased support for the Nazis was the fear, especially among the middle classes, of a possible communist takeover.

The German Communist party, the KPD (*Kommunistische Partei Deutschlands*), gradually recovered from the failure of the Spartacist Revolt of 1919 and the death of Rosa Luxemburg and Karl Liebknecht (see page 14). In 1923, new KPD leader Ernst Thälmann abandoned the goal of immediate revolution and from 1924 onwards contested Reichstag elections, with some success.

During the years of the Weimar Republic the KPD was the largest communist party in Europe, and was seen as the 'leading party' of the communist movement outside the Soviet Union. It maintained a solid electoral performance, usually polling more than 10 per cent of the vote, and gained 100 deputies in the November 1932 elections. In the presidential election of the same year, Thälmann took 13.2 per cent of the vote, compared to Hitler's 30.1 per cent (see page 44).

Source C KPD election poster from 1932. Translated, it reads 'Away with the system'

▼ Table 6.1 The role of the Reichstag and the President, 1930–32

	1930	1931	1932
Presidential decrees	5	44	66
Reichstag laws	98	34	5
Reichstag: days sitting	94	42	13

ACTIVITIES ?

1 Study Table 6.1. What does it show about democracy in Weimar Germany in the years 1930–32?

2 Study Source C. Why was the KPD attractive to many Germans?

6.2 Growth in support for the Nazis

The economic problems led to political discontent and meant extreme parties were able to secure support in the elections. In the period 1929–33, the Nazis became the largest political party in Germany. Hitler was able to appeal to all classes of society; his simple messages and slogans could be understood by all.

The role of Josef Goebbels

During the years 1929–33, the Nazis increased their support through propaganda. They did this in a variety of ways such as having mass rallies, putting up posters in prominent places and displaying banners wherever possible so that the Nazis appeared to be everywhere.

The Nazis were most fortunate in having a person who understood how to use the mass media and also to manipulate huge audiences. Josef Goebbels ensured that the Nazi message was simple and frequently repeated. By the early 1930s, the Nazis owned 120 daily or weekly newspapers regularly read by hundreds of thousands of people across the country. As Germany descended into political chaos in 1930–32, Goebbels was able to present the Nazi Party in local, regional, national and presidential elections. The Nazi message was heard everywhere, especially on the radio.

> **Source D** An extract from *Mein Kampf*, Hitler's autobiography
>
> Propaganda must confine itself to a very few points and repeat them endlessly. Here, as with so many things in this world, persistence is the first and foremost condition of success.

JOSEF GOEBBELS 1897–1945

1897	Born in Rheydt, now in North Rhine-Westphalia
1921	Left Heidelberg University after gaining a PhD in literature and philosophy
1922	Joined the Nazi Party
1927	Sets up his own newspaper, *Der Angriff* (*The Attack*)
1928	Elected to the Reichstag
1929	Appointed Head of Propaganda of the Nazi Party
1933	Appointed Minister for Propaganda and Popular Enlightenment

ACTIVITIES

1. Study Source D. How did Goebbels carry out Hitler's ideas on propaganda?
2. Study Source E. What message is the artist trying to put over to the German electorate?

◀ **Source E** Nazi Party election poster, 1930. The top reads: 'List 9 National Socialist German Workers' Party', and the snake is: moneylending, Versailles, unemployment, war, guilt, lie, Bolshevism, inflation and terror

Nazi electoral success

When Chancellor Heinrich Brüning called a general election in 1930, he was hoping to secure a clear majority for his Centre Party (ZP). However, the impact of the Wall Street Crash and the developing Depression disrupted the political situation. Unemployment had hit all classes and thus Hitler and the Nazis tried to appeal to all sections of society. The Nazi message was that Weimar had caused the economic crisis in Germany and the weak coalition governments had no real solutions to offer. The Nazis alone could unite Germany in a time of economic crisis.

The Nazis then played on the resentment of the Treaty of Versailles (see Source F). The old wounds were reopened and Germany's problems were blamed on the November Criminals and the Weimar Republic. Only the Nazis could restore Germany to its former glory.

> **Source F** Part of a speech made by Hitler in Munich, August 1923
>
> The day must come when a German government will summon up the courage to say to the foreign powers: 'The Treaty of Versailles is founded on a monstrous lie. We refuse to carry out its terms any longer. Do what you will! If you want war, go and get it! Then we shall see if you can turn 70 million Germans into slaves!' Either Germany sinks … or else we dare to enter on the fight against death and the devil.

If there were any who doubted the simple Nazi messages, Hitler ensured that another scapegoat could be offered. He blamed the Jews for Germany's problems. He said that they:

- were involved not only with Communism but also the evils of capitalism
- had helped to cause unemployment
- had conspired in Germany's defeat in the First World War
- had been involved in the Bolshevik Revolution
- were preparing to cause a revolution in Germany which would mean that all private property and wealth would be seized by the state.

The 1930 election proved to be the breakthrough for Hitler and the Nazi Party. For Brüning, the election meant that he still had to rely on other parties and, moreover, he continued to rely on Hindenburg and Article 48 (see page 41).

▼ Table 6.2 Reichstag seats after the elections of May 1928 and September 1930

Political party	Political position	May 1928	September 1930
Social Democratic Party (SPD)	Moderate	153	143
National Party (DNVP)	Right-wing	73	41
Nazi Party (NSDAP)	Right-wing	12	107
Centre Party (ZP)	Moderate	62	68
Communist Party (KPD)	Left-wing	54	77
People's Party (DVP)	Right-wing	45	30
Democratic Party (DDP)	Left-wing	25	20

ACTIVITY

Study Table 6.2. Write a brief newspaper article to show the main change in voting. In your article, suggest reasons for the electoral success of the Nazis.

Practice question

Give two things you can infer from Source D about Hitler and propaganda. (*For guidance, see page 78.*)

The presidential election of 1932

During the presidential election of 1932, when Hitler stood against Hindenburg, the Nazis were quick to use modern technology. For example, by using an aeroplane Hitler was able to speak at as many as five cities on the same day, flying from one venue to the next as indicated by the image chosen for the cover of the book about the campaign (see Source G). Goebbels ensured that there were mass rallies and that not only was the Nazi message being spread, but also that Hitler was being recognised as a national political figure. The message was proclaimed in films, on the radio and even records. Goebbels mastered the art of propaganda in these years. President Hindenburg did not campaign.

Hindenburg failed by a slight margin to win more than 50 per cent of the votes in the election so there had to be a second round. Hitler was successful in winning a large number of votes in each round, though he himself was quite disappointed at his showing. Goebbels presented the presidential defeat as a victory because of the huge vote for Hitler and the overall percentage of votes won.

▲ **Source G** The cover of the book *Hitler über Deutschland* (*Hitler over Germany*), published in Germany in 1932. This book was written shortly after Hitler had flown to five different cities to give speeches

ACTIVITY ?

What can you learn from Source G about Hitler's campaigning methods in the early 1930s?

Candidate	First round	Second round
Hindenburg	18,650,000	19,360,000
Hitler (NSDAP)	11,340,000	13,420,000
Thälmann (KPD)	4,968,000	3,710,000

▲ Figure 6.3 Results of the presidential election: first round, March 1932 and second round, April 1932

PAUL VON HINDENBURG 1846–1934

1846 Born in Posen (now Poznan, Poland)

1866 Joined the Prussian army

1870 (to 1871) Fought in the Franco–Prussian War

1903 Reached the rank of general

1914 Commanded German armies in East Prussia. Victorious at the Battles of Tannenberg and Masurian Lakes

1916 Made Chief of General Staff

1918 Retired from the army

1919 Put forward the *Dolchstoss* theory (see page 12)

1925–34 President of Germany

The tactics used by Hitler and Goebbels were paying off and there was greater success in the Reichstag elections in July 1932 (see page 49). Goebbels ensured that the German people were given positive images of Hitler and the Nazis. He also continued to play on their fears, particularly the fear of communism.

ACTIVITIES

1 In what ways do Source G and Source H support each other about the reasons why people voted for Hitler?

2 Read pages 42–45, then look at the table below. Complete the boxes, giving at least one reason to show how the Nazis could appeal to different groups of society at the same time.

Social group	How Nazis could appeal to them
Working classes	
Farmers	
Middle classes	
Upper classes	
Industrialists	

Financial support for the Nazis

Hitler and the Nazis could not have conducted their campaigns without financial backers. One example of how funds were crucial came in 1932, when 600,000 copies of the Nazi economic programme were produced and distributed in the July Reichstag election. The Nazi Party received funds from leading industrialists such as Thyssen, Krupp and Bosch. These industrialists were terrified of the communist threat and also concerned at the growth of trade union power. They knew that Hitler hated communism and that he would reduce the influence of the unions.

By 1932, the Nazis began to develop close links with the National Party (DNVP). The DNVP leader, Alfred Hugenberg, was a newspaper tycoon, and permitted the Nazis to publish articles which attacked Brüning. Hence, Goebbels continued the nationwide campaign against Weimar and keep the Nazis in the forefront of people's minds.

Practice question

Give two things you can infer from Source I about support for Hitler in the 1930s. (*For guidance, see page 78.*)

▲ **Source H** A Nazi poster of 1932. It says 'We farmers are getting rid of the dung' and 'We are voting Nazi'. The dung represents Jews and Socialists

Source I An anti-Hitler poster by a communist, John Heartfield. Born Helmut Herzfeld, he changed his name as a protest against the Nazis. He fled Germany in 1933. The caption reads 'The meaning of the Hitler salute. Motto: millions stand behind me! Little man asks for big gifts' ▶

ACTIVITIES ?

1 Look at Source J. Explain why it was important for Hitler to have the SA involved in battles with the communists.

2 What can you learn from Source K about the German Communist Party at this time?

The SA and the Communists

In his speeches, Hitler claimed that parliamentary democracy did not work and said that only he and the NSDAP could provide the strong government that Germany needed. The Nazis used the *Sturmabteilung* (SA) (see page 32) not only to provide protection for their meetings but also to disrupt the meetings of their opponents, especially the Communist Party. Hitler reappointed Ernst Röhm as leader of the SA in January 1931 and within a year its membership had increased by 100,000 to 170,000.

The Communists had their own private militia, the *Roter Frontkämpferbund* (Red Front Fighters, RFB), and there were countless fights between them and the SA. On many occasions there were fatalities. Hitler sought to show the German people that he could stamp out the Bolshevik violence and their threat of revolution. The SA also attacked and intimidated any overt opponents of the Nazis.

Source J A battle between ▶ SA members and communist RFB members in 1932. The signs read: 'Up the Revolution' and 'Free the political prisoners'

Source K Ernst Thälmann, ▶ leader of the German Communist Party, speaking at an open-air meeting in Berlin, 1932

The role of Hitler in increasing support for the Nazis

Hitler had developed the art of public speaking in the early days of the NSDAP and his speeches always attracted many people and helped increase the membership of the Nazi Party. He helped to draw up the Twenty-Five Point Programme (see page 31) and he was fully aware that after the Putsch he had to present himself and his party as law-abiding and democratic. He also knew that he had to be able to offer something to all groups in German society if he was to be successful in any elections. He never lost sight of these points during the two years before he became leader of Germany.

> **Source L** From *Inside the Third Reich* by Albert Speer, 1970. Speer was recalling a meeting in Berlin in 1930 at which Hitler spoke. Speer was a university lecturer and became Minister of Armaments in Nazi Germany
>
> I was carried away on a wave of enthusiasm [by the speech] … the speech swept away any scepticism, any reservations. Opponents were given no chance to speak … Here, it seemed to me, was hope. Here were new ideals, a new understanding, new tasks. The peril of communism, which seemed inevitably on its way, could be stopped. Hitler persuaded us that, instead of hopeless unemployment, Germany could move to economic recovery.

▲ **Source M** This a colourised photo of Hitler attending the Third Annual Nazi Party rally in Nuremberg, 1927

Hitler's charisma

Hitler could be all things to all people. He was the war hero, the saviour and the ordinary man in the street. The image created was that his whole existence was given over to Germany and there were no distractions to prevent him achieving his goals. He had created a philosophy which all could comprehend and furthermore his vision of the future revolved around making Germany the strongest nation in the world. Hitler had the one characteristic which most other politicians lacked – charisma.

> **Source N** Adapted from the diary of Luise Solmitz, 23 March 1932. A schoolteacher, Solmitz was writing about attending a meeting in Hamburg at which Hitler spoke
>
> There stood Hitler in a simple black coat, looking over the crowd of 120,000 people of all classes and ages ... a forest of swastika flags unfurled, the joy of this moment showed itself in a roaring salute ... The crowd looked up to Hitler with touching faith, as their helper, their saviour, their deliverer from unbearable distress ... He is the rescuer of the scholar, the farmer, the worker and the unemployed.

Practice questions

1 How useful are Sources N and O for an enquiry into the role of Hitler in increasing support for the Nazis in the years 1929–32? Explain your answer using Sources N and O and your knowledge of the historical context. (*For guidance, see pages 62–64.*)
2 Explain why there was increased support for the Nazis in the years 1929–32.

> You may use the following in your answer:
> ■ Unemployment
> ■ Goebbels
> You must also use information of your own.

(*For guidance, see pages 94–95.*)

ACTIVITIES ?

1 Study Sources L, M (on page 47) and N. What do these sources show you about Hitler and the Nazi Party?
2 Study Source O. Why would the Nazi Party want this image to be shown all over Germany?

Source O A portrait of Hitler painted in 1933 by B. von Jacobs ▶

6.3 Political developments in 1932

Political instability and the eventual, reluctant support of President Hindenburg brought Hitler to power as Chancellor in January 1933.

You have already seen that Hitler was quite successful in the presidential elections in March and April 1932. He was by now the leader of the second largest party in the Reichstag and was well known across Germany. When a general election was called for 31 July 1932, the Nazis were optimistic about improving on the number of votes they had won in the previous election of September 1930.

Brüning had been Chancellor since March 1930 but had little support in the Reichstag and was dependent on rule by presidential decree. His dependence on Hindenburg seriously weakened the Weimar Republic. By May 1932, he had lost the support of the President because of his failure to improve the economy. Hindenburg also opposed Brüning's scheme to give away bankrupt farms in Prussia to the unemployed.

There was much violence in the run up to the election. About 100 people were killed and more than 1,125 wounded in clashes between the political parties. On 17 July there were at least 19 people killed in Hamburg during a party rally.

More people voted in July than in any previous Weimar election. The Nazis won 230 seats and were now the largest party in the Reichstag (see Table 6.3). However, Franz von Papen of the Centre Party, despite not having the most seats, did not relinquish his post as Chancellor and began to scheme with President Hindenburg. Hitler demanded the post of Chancellor and at a meeting in August, Hindenburg refused to contemplate Hitler for the role even if he did lead the largest party in the Reichstag.

It was not possible for any party to command a majority in the Reichstag and it was impossible to maintain a coalition. Papen dissolved the Reichstag in September and new elections were set for early November. Papen held the opinion that the Nazis were losing momentum and if he held on they would slowly disappear from the scene. He was correct about them losing momentum as the results of the election showed (see Table 6.4).

▼ Table 6.3 Results of the July 1932 general election

Political party	No. Reichstag seats	% of vote
Nazis (NSDAP)	230	37.4
Social Democrats (SPD)	133	21.6
Communist Party (KPD)	89	14.3
Centre Party (ZP)	75	12.5
National Party (DNVP)	37	5.9
People's Party (DVP)	7	1.2
Democratic Party (DDP)	4	1.0

▼ Table 6.4 November 1932 election results

Political party	Reichstag seats	% of vote
Nazis (NSDAP)	196	33.1
Social Democrats (SPD)	121	20.4
Communist Party (KPD)	100	16.9
Centre Party (ZP)	70	11.9
National Party (DNVP)	52	8.8
People's Party (DVP)	11	1.9
Democratic Party (DDP)	2	1.0

Interpretation 1 From *Adolf Hitler* by I. Kershaw, in 1998

At the meeting in August, Hindenburg refused Hitler the Chancellorship. He could not answer, he said, before God, his conscience and the Fatherland if he handed over the entire power of the government to a single party and one which was so intolerant towards those with different views.

FRANZ VON PAPEN 1879–1969

1879 Born in Werl, Westphalia

1913 Entered the diplomatic service as a military attaché to the German ambassador in Washington DC

1917 German army adviser to Turkey and also served as a major in the Turkish army in Palestine

1918 Left the German army in 1918. Entered politics and joined the Catholic Centre Party

1922 Elected to the Reichstag

1932 Appointed Chancellor, schemed with Hindenburg thinking Hitler and the Nazis could be manipulated

1933 Appointed Vice-Chancellor under Hitler. Assumed Hitler could be dominated

ACTIVITIES

1 Study Table 6.2 (page 43) and Tables 6.3 and 6.4. What were the main voting trends over the three general elections?

2 What does Interpretation 1 tell us about Hindenburg's attitude to the Nazi Party?

Political intrigue

However, Papen could not secure a majority in the Reichstag and, at the same time, Hitler continued to demand the post of Chancellor. Papen suggested abolishing the Weimar constitution and at this, Kurt von Schleicher, the Minister of Defence, persuaded Hindenburg that if this happened there might be civil war. Papen lost Hindenburg's confidence and resigned. He was succeeded by Schleicher (translated, his name means 'sneaky', 'furtive' or 'intriguer'), who hoped to attain a majority in the Reichstag by forming a *Querfront*, meaning 'cross-front', whereby he would bring together different strands from left and right parties.

Papen was determined to regain power and to this end he met Hitler in early January 1933 and they agreed that Hitler should lead a Nazi-Nationalist government with Papen as the Vice-Chancellor. Intrigue and trickery now took the place of considered, open political debate. The army, major landowners and leaders of industry were convinced that Papen and Hitler were saving Germany from Schleicher's plans and a possible communist takeover. Papen was able to convince President Hindenburg that a coalition government with Hitler as Chancellor would save Germany and bring stability to the country. Papen said that he would be able to control Hitler – he would 'make Hitler squeak'.

On 30 January 1933, Adolf Hitler became Chancellor of Germany. He was the leader of the largest party and he had been invited to be leader by the President. He had achieved his aim of becoming Chancellor by legal and democratic means.

THE TEMPORARY TRIANGLE.

VON HINDENBURG AND VON PAPEN (*together*)—
"FOR HE'S A JOLLY GOOD FELLOW,
FOR HE'S A JOLLY GOOD FELLOW,
FOR HE'S A JOLLY GOOD FE-EL-LOW,
(*Aside:* "Confound him!")
AND SO SAY BOTH OF US!"

▲ **Source P** Cartoon from the British magazine *Punch*, January 1933

KURT VON SCHLEICHER 1882–1934

1882 Born in Brandenburg, Germany, the son of a Prussian army officer

1900 Joined the German army

1914–18 Worked as a general under the overall commander, Paul von Hindenburg

1925 Hindenburg elected president and Schleicher became his political adviser

1930 Persuaded Hindenburg to appoint Brüning as Chancellor

1932 Played a leading role in the removal of Papen and, in December, became Chancellor

1933 January Forced to resign as Chancellor

1934 June Murdered on the Night of the Long Knives

ACTIVITIES

1 Construct a timeline or flowchart to show the events for 1932 to January 1933.

2 Look at Source P. What do you think is meant by the term 'temporary triangle'?

3 Why do you think Papen thought he could control Hitler?

4 Reread pages 49–50, looking carefully at Source P and Interpretation 1. Copy the table below. In each cell write the main actions of the individual from mid-1932 to 1933.

Hitler	Papen	Schleicher	Hindenburg

6.4 How far do you agree with one of the interpretations?

This section provides guidance on how to answer the question 'How far do you agree with one of the interpretations?' Look at the question below:

Question

How far do you agree with Interpretation 2 about the extent of German recovery in the years 1924–29? Explain your answer, using both interpretations and your knowledge of the historical context.

Interpretation 1 From *Weimar and Nazi Germany*, F. Reynoldson, published in 1996

From 1924 to 1929 the Weimar Republic was much stronger than it had been just after the war. Led by Stresemann in the Reichstag, the different parties managed to work together. The extreme parties such as the Nazis gained fewer seats in the elections. The German people were better off and more contented. The Weimar Republic looked safe.

Interpretation 2 From *Weimar and Nazi Germany*, E. Wimlott, published in 1997

German prosperity was built on quicksand foundations. The Weimar economy was dependent upon high-interest American loans, which usually had to be repaid or renewed within three months. In times of depression, US moneylenders could demand rapid repayment. Moreover, unemployment never fell below 1.3 million. Although big business grew in the 1920s, small firms struggled and many went bankrupt.

How to answer

You need to give a balanced answer which agrees and disagrees with the interpretation using evidence from both interpretations as well as your own knowledge. An example is given below:

Step 1
State the view given in Interpretation 2 using evidence from the Interpretation itself.

> Interpretation 2 supports the view that the recovery of 1924-29 was built on weak foundations because it left Germany too dependent on the USA for loans and unemployment remained high.

Step 2
Agree with the view given in Interpretation 2 using your own knowledge. In answer to this question you would need to expand on the example answer with at least one more example of evidence from your own knowledge.

> It was certainly the case that the recovery of the Republic was too dependent on the USA, and when the American stock market collapsed in 1929, it had disastrous effects for Germany. Not everyone shared in the recovery. The lower middle class, whose occupations ranged from skilled craftspeople to newer jobs in the civil service, commerce and small businesses, did not fully recover from the hyperinflation of 1923. They felt that their interests were being ignored by the Weimar Republic.

Step 3
Disagree with the view given in Interpretation 2 using evidence from Interpretation 1. In answer to this question you would need to expand on the example answer with at least one more example of evidence from Interpretation 1.

> Interpretation 1 challenges the view that the recovery of 1924-29 was built on weak foundations because it suggests that the German people were better off and economic recovery led to political stability.

Step 4
Disagree with the view given in Interpretation 2 using your own knowledge. See if you can add to the example given with more evidence from your own knowledge.

> With money flowing in from America the economy seemed to prosper. Public works provided new stadiums, apartment blocks and opera houses. Big business had benefited from hyperinflation and had been able to pay off many of its debts and benefited from a period of industrial growth. Workers were generally better off during this period as wages increased and the average working day remained at eight hours.

Step 5
You now need to make a final judgement on the view given in Interpretation 2.

> Overall, I agree (or disagree) with Interpretation 2 because ...

6.5 Further examination practice on interpretations

Here is an opportunity to practise answering some more interpretation questions.

Interpretation 1 From a history textbook, *GCSE Modern World History*, B. Walsh, published in 1996

The Nazis won increased support after 1929 due to Hitler. He was their greatest campaigning asset. He was a powerful speaker and was years ahead of his time as a communicator. He travelled by plane on a hectic tour of rallies all over Germany. He appeared as a dynamic man of the moment, the leader of a modern party with modern ideas. At the same time, he was able to appear to be the man of the people, someone who knew and understood the people and their problems. Nazi supported rocketed.

Interpretation 2 From a history textbook, *Modern World History*, T. Hewitt, J. McCabe and A. Mendum, published in 1999

The Depression was the main reason for increased support for the Nazis. The government was taken by surprise at the speed and extent of the Depression. It also had very few answers as to how to deal with it. The Depression brought out all the weaknesses of the Weimar Republic, which seemed to be incapable of doing anything to end it. It is not surprising that the German people began to listen to parties promising to do something. In particular, they began to look to and support the Nazis.

Source A From 'A fairytale of Christmas', a short story written in 1931, by Rudolf Leonhard, a member of the Communist Party (KPD). Leonhard was writing about the unemployed in Germany

No one knew how many of them there were. They completely filled the streets … They stood or lay about in the streets as if they had taken root there. The streets were grey, their faces were grey, and even the hair on their heads and the stubble on the cheeks of the youngest there was grey with dust and their adversity.

Source B Adapted from the diary of Luise Solmitz, 23 March 1932. A schoolteacher, Solmitz was writing about attending a meeting in Hamburg at which Hitler spoke

There stood Hitler in a simple black coat, looking over the crowd of 120,000 people of all classes and ages … a forest of swastika flags unfurled, the joy of this moment showed itself in a roaring salute... The crowd looked up to Hitler with touching faith, as their helper, their saviour, their deliverer from unbearable distress … He is the rescuer of the scholar, the farmer, the worker and the unemployed.

Question 1

Study Interpretations 1 and 2. They give two views about the reasons for increased support for the Nazis in the years 1929–32. What is the main difference between the views? Explain your answer, using details from both interpretations.

- You need to give the views of each interpretation and back these up with evidence from each one.

Question 2

Suggest **one** reason why Interpretations 1 and 2 give different views about the reasons for increased support for the Nazis in the years 1929–32. You may use Sources A and B to help explain your answer.

The interpretations may differ because:

- they have given weight to two different sources. You can use evidence from Sources A and B for this answer. Match the sources to the interpretations
- they are partial extracts and in this case they do not actually contradict one another
- the authors have a different emphasis.

Question 3

How far do you agree with Interpretation 2 about the reasons for increased support for the Nazis in the years 1929–32? Explain your answer, using both interpretations and your knowledge of the historical context.

You need to give a balanced answer which agrees and disagrees with the interpretation using evidence from the two interpretations as well as your own knowledge.

- State the view given in Interpretation 2 using evidence from the Interpretation itself.
- Agree with the view given in Interpretation 2 using your own knowledge.
- Disagree with the view given in Interpretation 2 using evidence from Interpretation 1.
- Disagree with the view given in Interpretation 2 using your own knowledge.
- Make a final judgement on the view given in Interpretation 2.

Nazi control and dictatorship, 1933–39

This key topic examines the period from Hitler's appointment as Chancellor to his creation of the position of Führer in August 1934. It analyses how Hitler established the legal foundations of his dictatorship, removed any potential threats to his position, even from within the Nazi Party, and put in place methods of propaganda and censorship to persuade and encourage all German people to support Nazi ideals.

Each chapter within this key topic explains a key issue and examines important lines of enquiry as outlined in the boxes below.

There will also be guidance on how to answer the utility question (pages 62–64) and the inference question (page 78).

CHAPTER 7 THE CREATION OF A DICTATORSHIP AND THE POLICE STATE, 1933–34

- The Reichstag Fire, the Enabling Act and the banning of other parties and trade unions.
- The threat from Röhm and the SA, the Night of the Long Knives and the death of Hindenburg. Hitler becomes Führer, the army and the oath of allegiance.

CHAPTER 9 OPPOSITION, RESISTANCE AND CONFORMITY IN NAZI GERMANY

- The extent of support for the Nazi regime.
- Opposition from the Churches including the role of Pastor Niemöller.
- Opposition from the young including the Swing Youth and the Edelweiss Pirates.

CHAPTER 8 CONTROLLING AND INFLUENCING ATTITUDES

- The role of the Gestapo, the SS, the SD and concentration camps.
- Nazi control of the legal system, judges and law courts.
- Goebbels and the Ministry of Propaganda: censorship, Nazi use of media, rallies and sport, including the Berlin Olympics of 1936.
- Nazi control of the arts, including art, architecture, literature and film.
- Nazi policies towards the Catholic and Protestant Churches, including the Reich Church and Concordat.

TIMELINE

1933 January	Hitler becomes Chancellor	**1934 June**	Night of the Long Knives
1933 February	Reichstag fire	**1934 August**	President Hindenburg dies
1933 March	Nazi Party wins 288 seats in the general election	**1934 August**	Hitler combines posts of Chancellor and President, and assumes the title of Führer
1933 March	Enabling Act passed	**1934 August**	German army swears allegiance to Hitler
1933 May	Trade unions banned	**1938**	Over the course of the year, Hitler removes 16 army generals from their positions
1933 July	Nazis become the only legal party in Germany		

In the period from January 1933 to August 1934, Hitler and the Nazis secured control of all aspects of the German state. By August 1934, Hitler had combined the posts of Chancellor and President and was safe in the knowledge that the army supported him. Moreover, the banning of political parties, the control of the media, trade unions and police ensured that there was little or no opposition to the Nazi regime. Hitler pointed out that his actions were always within the legal framework of the time.

7.1 The importance of the Reichstag fire

ACTIVITY ?

Work in pairs. Source A shows the Reichstag on fire. What do you think the reactions would be if the Houses of Parliament in London burnt down? Explain your answer carefully. (Think about who people might blame and what people might want the government to do.)

When Hitler became Chancellor, there were only two other Nazis in the Cabinet of twelve – Wilhelm Frick and Hermann Goering. Frick was appointed Reich Minister for the Interior, which gave him power over government ministries and officials. Goering was Minister without Portfolio and also Minister for Prussia, and the latter post gave him control of nearly two-thirds of Germany. Hitler's position as Chancellor was not strong because the Nazis and his allies, the Nationalist Party, did not have a majority in the Reichstag. Furthermore, President Hindenburg detested him. However, it was soon clear that Papen's claim that he would be able to control Hitler (see page 50) was utterly wrong.

Hitler immediately called a general election for 5 March, hoping it would give him a clear majority in the Reichstag. If he controlled parliament then he would be able to make the laws that would be needed to tighten his grip on the nation. It would all be done by the rule of law – Nazi law. Violence and terror were again seen in this election campaign and there were about 70 deaths in the weeks leading up to voting day. Once again, Hitler received large amounts of money from leading industrialists to assist with his campaign, and with access to the media, he knew that Goebbels would be able to put the Nazi message over unceasingly. One week before the election, on 27 February, the Reichstag building was set on fire.

Source A The Reichstag (parliament) building on fire, 27 February 1933

It is not known who started the fire, but Marinus van der Lubbe, a Dutch Communist, was found at the scene of the fire and arrested. This was an ideal opportunity for Hitler and Goebbels to exploit. They claimed that van der Lubbe had started the fire and that the Communists were about to stage a takeover.

On the day following the fire, Hitler persuaded President Hindenburg to sign the 'Decree for the Protection of People and State'. The decree replaced the constitutional government by a permanent state of emergency and suspended basic civil rights. It allowed the Nazis to imprison large numbers of their political opponents. In the week after the fire, 4,000 Communist Party members were arrested including the leader, Ernst Thälmann. In addition, the SA killed 51 Nazi opponents and injured several hundred. The police did nothing. Communist and socialist newspapers were banned.

Source B From the memoirs of Rudolf Diels, head of the Prussian police in 1933. He was writing about Hitler's reaction to the Reichstag fire. Diels was writing in 1950

Hitler was standing on a balcony gazing at the red ocean of fire. He swung round towards us … his face had turned quite scarlet with the excitement … Suddenly he started screaming at the top of his voice: 'Now we'll show them! Anyone who stands in our way will be mown down. The German people have been too soft for too long. Every communist official must be shot. All friends of the Communists must be locked up. And that goes for the Social Democrats too.'

ACTIVITIES

1 Study Source B. What does this source tell you about Hitler's thoughts about the fire?
2 Study Source C. What impression of van der Lubbe do you gain from the photograph?
3 Devise a caption for Source C for publication in a Nazi newspaper.
4 Find out more about the background and trial of Marinus van der Lubbe.
5 What does Source D show about the role of the police in Berlin in March 1933?

▲ **Source C** Photograph of the trial of Marinus van der Lubbe. Van der Lubbe is wearing a striped jacket

▲ **Source D** Berlin police burn red flags after raiding the homes of Communists, 26 March 1933

7.2 The importance of the Enabling Act

In the election in March 1933 the Nazis won 288 seats (see Table 7.1). Despite the imprisoning of many of the Socialists and Communists and having all the advantages of media control, the Nazis did not win a majority of votes, even though they increased their vote by 5.5 million on the November election. Therefore, a coalition government was formed with the National Party (DNVP), ensuring a majority (51.9 per cent) in the Reichstag. Even having a majority, Hitler was disappointed because he needed two-thirds of the seats in order to be able to change the constitution.

▼ Table 7.1 Election results, March 1933

Political party	Reichstag seats	% of vote
Nazi Party (NSDAP)	288	43.9
National Party (DNVP)	52	8.0
People's Party (DVP)	2	1.1
Centre Party (ZP)	92	13.9
Democratic Party (DDP)	5	0.9
Social Democratic Party (SPD)	120	18.3
Communist Party (KPD)	81	12.3
Others	7	1.6

Hitler's next step was to pass the Enabling Act. This would give him and his government full powers for the next four years and would mean that the Reichstag would become a rubber stamp for Nazi activities. As Chancellor, Hitler would have greater powers than the President. The Enabling Act was passed but by devious means (see Figure 7.1). The Communist Party could not prevent the passing of the Act because its members were in jail and the Centre Party decided to support the Act because Hitler promised to respect the rights of the Catholic Church.

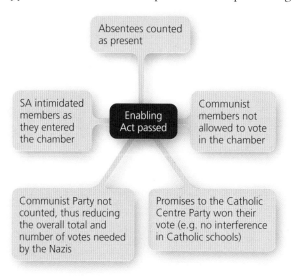

The Enabling Act became law on 24 March and this signalled the end of the Weimar constitution and democracy. Hitler could now move to secure closer control of the nation by means of this new law. It was renewed in 1937 and 1941.

◀ Figure 7.1 Summary of the passing of the Enabling Act

ACTIVITIES

1 Work in pairs. You are investigative journalists in Germany in 1933. Write an article exposing the links between the Reichstag fire (pages 54–55) and how the Enabling Act was passed.

2 Give two things you can learn from Table 7.1 about the election results of March 1933.

7.3 The removal of opposition

With the new Enabling Act, Hitler was in a position to bring German society into line with Nazi philosophy. This policy was called *Gleichschaltung*. It would create a truly national socialist state and would mean that every aspect of the social, political and economic life of German citizens was controlled and monitored by the Nazis.

The end of trade unions

On 2 May 1933, all trade unions were banned. The Nazis said that a national community had been created and therefore such organisations were no longer needed. The Nazi German Labour Front (DAF) was set up to replace not only trade unions but also employers' groups. Wages were decided by the DAF and workers received workbooks, which recorded the record of employment. Employment depended on the ownership of a workbook. Strikes were outlawed and any dissenters would be sent to the new prisons – concentration camps – for political re-education. The first concentration camp opened at Dachau in March 1933. There could be no challenge to the Nazi state.

The banning of political parties

On 14 July 1933, the Law against the Formation of Parties was passed, which made the Nazi Party the sole legal political party in Germany. However, before this law was passed, the existing parties had experienced severe restrictions. The Communist Party members had not been allowed to take their seats in the Reichstag and property had been confiscated. On 10 May, the Socialist Party had its headquarters and other property seized. In June, the Socialists gave up their seats in the Reichstag and by the end of June, all the other parties had dissolved themselves. Germany was now a one-party state.

In the November 1933 general election, 95.2 per cent of the electorate voted and the Nazis won 39,638,000 votes. (There was some protest against the Nazis – about three million ballot papers were spoilt.)

The abolition of the *Länder*

Hitler also broke down the federal structure of Germany. There were eighteen *Länder* (districts), and each had its own parliament. On occasions in the Weimar period, some of the *Länder* had caused problems for the President because their political make-up differed and they refused to accept decisions made in the Reichstag. President Ebert had issued more than 130 emergency decrees to overrule some of the *Länder*. Hitler decided that the *Länder* were to be run by Reich governors and their parliaments were abolished in January 1934. Thus he centralised Germany for the first time since its creation in 1871.

ACTIVITIES

1 What is meant by the term *Gleichschaltung*?
2 Explain why *Gleichschaltung* was important for the Nazis.
3 Why was it important that Hitler banned trade unions and political parties?

▲ **Source E** SA members seizing trade union offices in Berlin, 2 May 1933

7.4 The importance of the Night of the Long Knives

The Night of the Long Knives (also known as 'Operation Hummingbird' or the 'Blood Purge') was the purging of Hitler's political and military rivals in the SA (*Sturmabteilung*). One cause of the removal of the leaders of the SA was the need to win the support of the army (see page 61). In addition, in the first months of his Chancellorship, Hitler saw the SA as a major threat.

The SA had played a key part in the growth of the Nazis and by 1933 they were well known across Germany. Most of the SA were working-class men who favoured the socialist views of the Nazi programme. They were hoping that Hitler would introduce reforms to help the workers.

During the first months of 1933 the SA had helped to create an atmosphere of terror and intimidation when *Gleichschaltung* was introduced. Some leading Nazis, such as Wilhelm Frick and Hermann Goering, felt that the activities of the SA might cause a backlash against Hitler and began to look for ways of controlling them (Source F). Goering was concerned that the army might step in. There was further tension because Ernst Röhm, leader of the SA, wanted to incorporate the army into the SA and was disappointed with Hitler's close relations with industrialists and the army leaders. Röhm wanted more government interference in the running of the country in order to help the ordinary citizens. He wanted to move away from Germany's class structure and bring greater equality. In effect, Röhm wanted a social revolution.

There was added tension for Hitler because his personal bodyguard, the SS (*Schutzstaffel*), led by Heinrich Himmler, wished to break away from the SA. Goering (head of the Gestapo) wanted to lead the armed forces and he too saw an opponent in Röhm.

> **Source F** From a report by Wilhelm Frick, Minister of the Interior, 6 October 1933
>
> Despite repeated announcements by the Reich Chancellor [Hitler], and despite numerous circulars, new infringements by subordinate leaders and by members of the SA have been reported again and again during the past weeks. Above all, SA leaders and SA men have carried out police actions for which they had no authority whatever … and which cannot be reconciled with the existing laws and regulations. These infringements must now stop.

▼ Table 7.2 Membership of uniformed services in early 1934

Service	Members (approx.)
Sturmabteilung (SA)	3,000,000
Schutzstaffel (SS)	52,000
Army	100,000

> **Source G** From comments made by Ernst Röhm to Kurt Lüdecke in January 1934. Lüdecke was a fundraiser for the Nazi Party and was a close friend of Röhm
>
> Hitler can't walk over me as he might have done a year ago; I've seen to that. Don't forget that I have three million men, with every key position in the hands of my own people, Hitler knows that I have friends in the *Reichswehr* [Germany's armed forces], you know! If Hitler is reasonable I shall settle the matter quietly; if he isn't I must be prepared to use force – not for my sake but for the sake of our revolution.

▲ **Source H** Photograph of Hitler and Röhm with SA troops. The flags are from different SA units across Germany.

The events of 30 June 1934

Hitler took action in June, following information from Himmler that Röhm was about to seize power. On 30 June 1934, Röhm and the main leaders of the SA (Karl Ernst and Edmund Hennes) were shot by members of the SS. Hitler also took the opportunity to settle some old scores: former Chancellor Kurt von Schleicher was murdered, as was Gregor Strasser, a key figure (and an old rival) among those Nazis with socialist views similar to Röhm. Figures vary, but it is thought that about 400 people were murdered in the purge.

> **Source I From a report of the Reich cabinet meeting about the Night of the Long Knives, printed in the *Völkischer Beobachter* (the official Nazi newspaper), 5 July 1934**
>
> Defence Minister General von Blomberg thanked the Führer in the name of the Reich Cabinet and the army for his determined and courageous action, by which he saved the German people from a civil war. The Führer had shown greatness as a statesman and a soldier. This had aroused in the hearts of … the German people a vow of service, devotion and loyalty in this grave hour.

> **Source J From Hitler's speech to the Reichstag on 13 July 1934, justifying his actions in the Night of the Long Knives concerning the SA**
>
> In the circumstances I had to make but one decision. If disaster was to be prevented at all, action had to be taken with lightning speed. Only a ruthless and bloody intervention might still perhaps stifle the spread of revolt. If anyone reproaches me and asks why I did not resort to the regular courts of justice for conviction of the offenders, then all I can say is, 'In this hour I was responsible for the fate of the German people and therefore I became the supreme judge of the German people.'

ACTIVITIES

1 What can you learn from Source F about the SA?

2 Look back at the Twenty-Five Point Programme on page 31 and the text about Röhm's ideas about a social revolution.
   a) Discuss in class with your teacher which parts of the programme match Röhm's views.
   b) Explain why Hitler and some of his industrialist supporters were concerned about Röhm.

3 Suggest reasons why Source I was published in the *Völkischer Beobachter*.

Practice questions

1 How useful are Sources F and G for an enquiry into the concerns Hitler had about the SA? Explain your answer, using Sources F and G and your knowledge of the historical context. *(For guidance, see pages 62–64.)*

2 Give two things you can infer from Source J about Hitler. *(For guidance, see page 78.)*

The impact of the Night of the Long Knives

The Night of the Long Knives is often seen as the turning point for Hitler's rule in Germany. He eradicated would-be opponents and secured the support of the army. The SA was relegated to a minor role and if there was any doubt about Hitler's rule, it was now clear that fear and terror would play significant roles.

THEY SALUTE WITH BOTH HANDS NOW.

▲ **Source K** A cartoon from the *London Evening Standard*, 3 July 1934. The caption reads: 'They salute with both hands now'. Goering is standing to Hitler's right dressed as a Viking hero and Goebbels is on his knees behind Hitler. The words 'Hitler's unkept promises' appear on the paper in front of the SA and 'the double cross' above and below Hitler's armband

▲ **Source L** A cartoon published in the *Daily Express*, 3 July 1934, shortly after the Night of the Long Knives. The caption is 'Will members of the audience kindly keep their seats'. Members of the audience include representatives from the USA, UK and the USSR

Practice question

Give two things you can infer from Source K about the Night of the Long Knives. *(For guidance, see page 78.)*

ACTIVITIES

1 What message is the cartoonist trying to put over in Source L?

2 What were the results of the Night of the Long Knives? Construct a circle with 'The Night of the Long Knives' at the centre. Look at the points below and consider the results of the purge for each, working out who gained most from the Night of the Long Knives and who gained the least, or lost. Then place them around the circle, starting with the one that benefited most at the top and working in a clockwise direction:

- the army
- the SA
- Hitler's rivals
- the SS
- Hitler's own position
- Himmler
- Goering

7.5 The support of the army

Hitler had been keen to secure the support of the army since his appointment as Chancellor. He was aware that army officers did not like the SA and that they viewed its activities with distaste. He began to think that if he removed the SA, he could win the support of the army in his bid for the presidency because the army felt threatened by the SA and many of the army leaders did not like its socialist nature. Hindenburg was becoming very frail and Hitler sought to combine his own post and that of President. The Night of the Long Knives (see page 58) was important for Hitler because the army leaders offered their support after the leaders of the SA were assassinated.

For Hitler, the purging of the SA was crucial because he had had his opponents murdered and there had been no opposition to his actions. As a result, he grew in confidence, especially when a law was passed on 3 July 1934 which stated that Hitler's actions during the Night of the Long Knives were legal.

On the death of Hindenburg in August 1934, the army swore allegiance to Hitler who, having combined the posts of Chancellor and President, was now their Führer (see Source M). Hitler decided he needed to seek the approval of the German people when he combined the posts. In the referendum that followed, more than 90 per cent of the voters (38 million) agreed with his action. Only four and a half million voted against him. With his new title, the support of the army and the resounding vote in the referendum, Hitler and the Nazi Party were in an extremely secure position.

> **Source M** The army's oath of allegiance to Hitler, August 1934
>
> I swear before God to give my unconditional obedience to Adolf Hitler, Führer of the Reich and of the German people, and I pledge my word as a brave soldier to observe this oath always, even at the peril of my life.

Source N Army recruits swearing the oath of allegiance to Hitler in a mass ceremony in Munich, 7 November 1935 ▶

ACTIVITIES ?

1 How helpful is Source M in helping you understand why Hitler felt more secure after the army oath had been made?

2 Look at Source N. Can you suggest reasons to explain why photographs such as this were displayed all over Germany?

3 What can you learn from Source O about support for Hitler in August 1934?

Source O Hitler Youth ▶ during the referendum on the merging of the offices of Reich President and Chancellor (19 August 1934). The words on the lorry read 'The Führer commands, we follow! Everyone say yes!'

7.6 The utility question

This section provides guidance on how to answer the question about utility.

In answering the utility question, you must analyse various aspects of two sources and, in order to reach the top level, you need to cover them all. The content and the nature, origin and purpose (NOP) of a source should be considered and out of this there will emerge an evaluation of the source's utility and reliability. In addition, you must also include knowledge of the historical context to support inferences and/or to assess the usefulness of information.

In order to reach higher level marks for this question you have to explain the value (usefulness) of both the content and the NOP of each source. The NOP is found in the provenance of the source – the information given above or below it. A good tip is to highlight or underline key words in the provenance which show either the utility or the limitations of the source. An example of this approach is given for Source A on page 63.

There is also guidance in the box below about what to consider for the NOP of a source.

NOP MEANS ...

N Nature of the source

What type of source is it? A speech, a photograph, a cartoon, a letter, an extract from a diary? How will the nature of the source affects its utility? For example, a private letter is often very useful because the person who wrote it generally gives their honest views.

O Origins of the source

Who wrote or produced the source? Are their views worth knowing? Are they giving a one-sided view? When was it produced? It could be an eyewitness account. What are the advantages and disadvantages of eyewitness accounts?

P Purpose of the source

For what reason was the source produced? For example, the purpose of adverts is to make you buy the products; people usually make speeches to get your support. How will this affect the utility of the source?

Question 1

How useful is Source A for an enquiry into the activities of the SA? Explain your answer, using Source A and your knowledge of the historical context.

How to answer

Although in the exam the question will be on two sources, in Question 1 we look at one source to help you build your skills in analysing a source. Question 2 on page 64 is about the utility of two sources.

First let us concentrate on content. For each source you should think about the following questions:

1   What is **useful** about the content of the source?
    ■   What does it mention? How useful is this compared to your own knowledge of the event? This is known as your contextual knowledge.
    ■   What view does it give about the feelings of people? Can you add any contextual knowledge to support your answer?

For example:

> Source A states that members of the SA have been breaking rules and regulations and exceeding their authority. This is useful because it begins to show why Hitler was concerned about the power of the SA. It is useful because it shows that leading Nazis like Frick wanted to be seen adhering to the law of the land – legality was important for Hitler at the beginning.

Now we will move on to NOP.

Page 63 shows examples of the values and limitations of the NOP of Source A as evidence of the activities of the SA.

Nature

It is useful because it is an official report which leads us to think it has some credibility and has been put together over some time. However, it is less useful because it has been written by a Nazi and the Nazis and Frick wanted to discredit the SA.

Source A From a report by Wilhelm Frick, Minister of the Interior, 6 October 1933

Despite repeated announcements by the Reich Chancellor [Hitler], and despite numerous circulars, new infringements by subordinate leaders and by members of the SA have been reported again and again during the past weeks. Above all, SA leaders and SA men have carried out police actions for which they had no authority whatsoever… and which cannot be reconciled with existing laws and regulations. These infringements must now stop.

Origins

It is useful because Frick was a senior Nazi who had access to information about events across Germany. However, it is less useful because it was written by someone close to Hitler who wanted to confirm Hitler's view of the SA. It would be typical of anti-SA propaganda.

Purpose

It is useful because it is an example of anti-SA propaganda which shows how the organisation was not taking notice of even Hitler. Its purpose was to show how the SA was acting illegally (which is what Hitler was at pains for the Nazis not to do). It is useful because it shows that even as late as October 1933, Hitler was not in complete control of Germany and needed to act with restraint. It is also useful because it informs us why Hitler began to have concerns about the SA. It is less useful because it is rather contradictory as SA members were drafted in as auxiliary policemen and were given wide powers during the early stages of Gleichschaltung. This lack of precision makes the source not only less useful about the SA's activities but also less reliable.

ACTIVITY

Now, have a go answering Question 1 using all the guidance given on these two pages. Make a copy of the planning grid below and use it to plan your answer. Include the value of the content of the source and any contextual knowledge to support that. Try also to add some contextual knowledge when you make a point in the NOP columns.

	Value	Contextual knowledge
Contents		
What does the source tell you?		
What view does the source give?		
NOP		
Nature		
Origin		
Purpose		

The utility of two sources

For this paper you will need to evaluate the utility of two sources.

Question 2

How useful are Sources B and C for an enquiry into the Reichstag fire? Explain your answer, using Sources B and C and your knowledge of the historical context.

Source B From the memoirs of Rudolf Diels, Head of the Prussian police in 1933. He was writing about Hitler's reaction to the Reichstag fire. Diels arrived at the Reichstag soon after it had been set on fire on 27 February 1933. He wrote his memoirs in 1950

Shortly after my arrival at the burning Reichstag, the National Socialist leaders arrived. Hitler was standing on a balcony gazing at the red ocean of fire. As I entered, Goering came towards me. His voice was heavy with the emotion: 'This is the beginning of the Communist revolt, they will start their attack now! Not a moment must be lost.' Hitler turned to the assembled company. Now I saw that his face was purple with agitation and with the heat. He shouted uncontrollably, as I had never seen him do before, as if he was going to burst: 'There will be no mercy now. Anyone who stands in our way will be cut down. Every communist official will be shot where he is found. Everybody in league with the Communists must be arrested. There will also no longer be leniency for Social Democrats.'

Source C From *My Part in Hitler's Fight* by Joseph Goebbels, written in 1935

Hitler came to supper at 9 p.m. Suddenly, the telephone rang. The Reichstag is burning! I thought the news was pure fantasy and, at first, did not inform the Führer. After a few more calls, I was able to confirm that the terrible news was true ... We raced to the scene at top speed. Goering met us and soon Papen arrived. It had already been established that the fire was due to arson. There could be no doubt that the Communists had made a final attempt to seize power by creating an atmosphere of panic and terror.

How to answer

- Explain the value of the contents of each source and try to add some contextual knowledge when you make a point.
- Explain the value of the NOP of each source and try to add some contextual knowledge when you make a point.

Make a copy of the following grid to plan your answer for each source, and use the writing frame below.

Source B	Value	Contextual knowledge
Nature		
Origins		
Purpose		
Content		

Source B is useful because it suggests (contents) ....

This is supported by my contextual knowledge ....

Moreover Source B is also useful because of (NOP) ....

This is supported by my contextual knowledge ....

Source C is useful because it suggests (contents) ....

This is supported by my contextual knowledge ....

Moreover Source C is also useful because of (NOP) ....

This is supported by my contextual knowledge ....

8 Controlling and influencing attitudes

A key element in maintaining a Nazi dictatorship was to create a climate of fear – make people too frightened to actively oppose the Nazi state. This was achieved through the establishment of a police state, including a secret police (the Gestapo), the SS, an intelligence agency (the *Sicherheitsdienst,* Security Service), Nazi control of the law courts and the setting up of concentration camps. Moreover, Hitler was determined to reduce the influence of the German Catholic and Protestant Churches because Christian ideas contrasted greatly with those of the Nazi Party.

8.1 The development of the Nazi police state

You have read earlier how the Nazis wanted to control all aspects of German life and used the policy of *Gleichschaltung* (see page 57) in order to achieve this. If indoctrination did not work, then force and terror were used. The Nazis used their own organisations to instil fear into the people. The SS (*Schutzstaffel*), SD (*Sicherheitsdienst*) and Gestapo were the main ones and in 1936 they were all brought under the control of Himmler.

ACTIVITY ?

What does Source A suggest about Nazi police methods?

▼ **Source A** German citizens being searched in the street by Gestapo officers and armed uniformed police, 1933

The role of the SS (*Schutzstaffel*)

The SS had been formed in 1925 to act as a bodyguard unit for Hitler and was led by Himmler after 1929. Himmler built up the SS until it had established a clear visible identity – members wore black. They showed total obedience to the Führer. By 1934 the SS had more than 50,000 members who were to be fine examples of the Aryan race and were expected to marry racially pure wives. Membership of the SS and its various bodies had grown to 250,000 by 1939.

After the Night of the Long Knives (see page 58), the SS became responsible for the removal of all opposition within Germany. Within the SS, the Security Service (SD) (see page 67) had the task of maintaining security within the party and then the country.

> **Source B** From a speech by Himmler to the Committee for Police Law at the Academy of German Law, 1936
>
> Right from the start, I have taken the view that it does not matter in the least if our actions are against some clause in the law; in my work for my Führer and the nation, I do what my conscience and common sense tell me is right.

> **Interpretation 1** An extract from *Documents on Nazism 1919–45* by J. Noakes and G. Pridham, written in 1974
>
> Hitler needed an organisation which would not feel restrained by the law. It would act with utter ruthlessness and would be dedicated to expressing his will and the ideas of the Nazi movement. He found what he needed in the SS.

> **Interpretation 2** An extract from *Years of Weimar and the Third Reich* by D. Evans and J. Jenkins , published in 1999
>
> The SS members were totally dedicated to what they regarded as the supreme virtues of Nazi ideology – loyalty and honour. They saw themselves as the protectors of the Aryan way of life and the defenders of the people against agitators, the criminal classes and those they saw as being responsible for the Jewish–Communist threat.

HEINRICH HIMMLER 1900–45

1900 Born near Munich

1918 Joined the army

1923 Joined the Nazi Party and participated in the Munich Putsch

1929 Appointed leader of the SS

1930 Elected as a member of parliament

1934 Organised the Night of the Long Knives

1936 Head of all police agencies in Germany

1945 Committed suicide

The Gestapo

The Gestapo (*Geheimestaatspolizei* – secret state police) was set up in 1933 by Goering and in 1936 it came under the control of Himmler and the SS. By 1939, the Gestapo was the most important police section of the Nazi state. It could arrest and imprison those suspected of opposing the state. The most likely destination would be a concentration camp run by the SS. It has been estimated that, by 1939, there were about 160,000 people under arrest for political crimes.

> **Source C** Hermann Goering *Germany Reborn*, written in 1934 explaining his role in setting up the Gestapo
>
> Finally, I alone created, on my own initiative, the State Secret Police Department. This is the instrument which is so much feared by the enemies of the State, and which is chiefly responsible for the fact that in Germany and Prussia today there is no question of a Marxist or Communist danger.

> **Source D** An incident reported in the Rhineland, July 1938
>
> In a cafe, a 64-year-old woman remarked to her companion at the table: 'Mussolini [leader of Italy] has more political sense in one of his boots than Hitler has in his brain.' The remark was overheard and five minutes later the woman was arrested by the Gestapo, who had been alerted by telephone.

ACTIVITIES

1 What can you learn from from Interpretation 1 about the SS?

2 Why did Hitler want to create such an elite organisation as the SS? (*For guidance see pages 94–95.*)

3 In pairs, discuss why Hitler allowed so many different security organisations – Gestapo, SS and SD.

Practice questions

1 How far do you agree with Interpretation 2 about the role of the SS in the Nazi police state? Explain your answer using both interpretations and your own knowledge of the historical context. (*For guidance, see page 51.*)

2 Give two things you can infer from Source D about life in Germany under the Nazis. (*For guidance, see page 78.*)

The *Sicherheitsdienst* (SD)

The *Sicherheitsdienst* (SD) was set up in 1931 as the intelligence body of the Nazi Party and was under the command of Himmler. Himmler appointed a former naval officer, Reinhard Heydrich, to organise the department. The main aim of the SD was to discover actual and potential enemies of the Nazi Party and ensure that they were then removed.

Members of the SD were employed by the Nazi Party, which paid their salaries. The SD attracted many professional and highly educated people such as lawyers, economists and professors of politics.

The concentration camps

As soon as the Enabling Act had been passed (see page 57), the Nazis established a new kind of prison – a concentration camp – to confine those whom they deemed to be their political, ideological and racial opponents. At first, concentration camps were set up to detain political opponents including Communists, Socialists, trade unionists, and others who had left-wing and liberal political views. In 1939 there were more than 150,000 people under arrest for political offences.

The SD and SS ran the concentration camps though only the Gestapo had the authority to carry out arrests or interrogations and send people there. The earliest of these camps was in Dachau, near Munich. Others followed, including at Buchenwald, Mauthausen and Sachsenhausen.

Prisoners were classified into different categories, each denoted by a different-coloured triangle which had to be worn. For example, those who wore black triangles were vagrants and 'work-shy', pink triangles denoted homosexual people and red triangles were for political prisoners (see Figure 8.2).

Initially, work in the camps was hard and pointless, like breaking stones, but gradually the prisoners were used as forced workers in quarries, construction, coal mines and armament factories.

The camp inmates were underfed and treated with great brutality and mortality rates were very high. If someone was killed at a concentration camp family members would receive a note saying that the inmate had died of a disease or been shot trying to escape.

▲ Figure 8.1 The position of some concentration camps in 1933–39

ACTIVITIES

1 Study Figure 8.1. What can you learn from the map about the importance of concentration camps in Nazi Germany?

2 Study figure 8.2. Why do you think the prisoners were separated into different categories?

Religious groups
Known as the *Bibelforscher* (bible students); included Catholics and Protestants who opposed the Nazi regime

Political prisoners
Included Communists, members of other political parties and trade union leaders

Foreign forced-labour groups
Non-German ethnic groups who were seen as a threat to the Nazi regime

Different categories of prisoners

The 'work-shy'
Included anyone unwilling to work, as well as Gypsies, the homeless and alcoholicsxt

Sexual offenders

Professional criminals
Included burglars and thieves

Jews
Regularly rounded up but in much greater numbers after Kristallnacht (see page 108)

Figure 8.2 Different categories of prisoners ▶

Source E Edward Adler, a survivor, describes his journey to and arrival at Sachsenhausen concentration camp in 1934

One particular incident I recall like it was yesterday. An old gentleman with the name of Solomon, I'll never forget. He must have been well into his seventies. He simply couldn't run. He couldn't run and he collapsed, and he laid in the road, and one of the storm troopers stepped on his throat. This is true. Unbelievable, but true, 'til the man was dead. We had to pick up his body and throw him to the side of the road, and we continued on into the camp, where we were assembled in a courtyard, and a strange incident happened at that time. We faced a barrack, a door on the right, a door on the left. People went in the left door, came out the right door, entirely different people. Their hair was shaven off, they had a prisoner's uniform on, a very wide, striped uniform. My number was 6199.

Practice questions

1 Give two things you can infer from Source E about the treatment of prisoners in concentration camps. (*For guidance, see page 78.*)
2 Explain why the police state was a success in removing opposition to the Nazi regime.

You may use the following in your answer:
- Concentration camps
- The Gestapo

You must also use information of your own.

(*For guidance, see pages 94–95.*)

▲ **Source F** The arrival of prisoners at Oranienburg concentration camp in 1933

8.2 The Nazi control of the legal system

Even though the Nazis controlled the Reichstag and could make laws, Hitler wanted to ensure that all laws were interpreted in a Nazi fashion. The law courts therefore had to experience *Gleichschaltung*, just as any other part of society. Some judges were removed and all had to become members of the National Socialist League for the Maintenance of Law (NSRB). This meant that Nazi views were upheld in the courts. In October 1933, the German Lawyers Front was established and there were more than 10,000 members by the end of the year. The lawyers had to swear that they would 'strive as German jurists to follow the course of our Führer to the end of our days'.

From 1936, judges had to wear the swastika and Nazi eagle on their robes (see Source G).

ACTIVITY ?

Study Source G. Devise two captions for the photograph, one that could have been used by a supporter of the Nazis and one by an opponent.

▲ **Source G** Judge Roland Freisler, State Secretary at the Reich Ministry of Justice. Here, he is presiding over a People's Court (see page 70)

The Protestant Church

There were some Protestants who admired Hitler. They were called 'German Christians'. They established a new Reich Church, hoping to combine all Protestants under one Church. Their leader was Ludwig Müller, who was a member of the NSDAP and became the Reich Bishop (*Reichsbischof*), the Church's national leader, in September 1933.

> **Source N** A Protestant pastor speaking in a 'German Christian' church in 1937
>
> We all know that if the Third Reich were to collapse today, communism would come in its place. Therefore we must show loyalty to the Führer who has saved us from communism and given us a better future. Support the 'German Christian' Church.

However, many Protestants opposed Nazism, which they believed conflicted greatly with their own Christian beliefs. They were led by Pastor Martin Niemöller (see page 82), a First World War submarine commander. In December 1933 they set up the Pastors' Emergency League for those who opposed Hitler.

> **Interpretation 1** From *Nazi Germany* by J. Cloake (OUP), published in, 1997
>
> The Nazis never destroyed the established Churches in Germany. They made it difficult for Christians to worship but the churches remained open and services were held. However, Hitler succeeded in his aim of weakening the Churches as a source of resistance to his policies.

ACTIVITIES

1 Study Source N. This speech was widely publicised by the Nazis. Why?
2 Study Source O. You are an opponent of the new Reich Protestant Church. Devise a caption for this photograph.
3 What can you learn from Interpretation 1 about Nazi policies towards the Churches?

Practice questions

1 How useful are Sources N and P for an enquiry into the attitudes of the Nazis to the Christian Church? (*For guidance see pages 62–64.*)
2 Explain why the Nazis tried to control the Church in Germany. (*For guidance, see pages 94–95.*)

You may use the following in your answer:
■ Roman Catholic Church
■ German Faith Movement

You must also use information of your own.

▲ **Source O** *Reichsbischof* Müller after the consecration of the Gustav Adolf Church as a Reich church, Berlin, 1933

Zur Gründung der deutschen Staatskirche

Das Kreuz war noch nicht schwer genug

▲ **Source P** A protest poster by John Heartfield, a communist artist who opposed the Nazis. The words translate to 'The cross wasn't heavy enough'

8.4 Goebbels and the Ministry of Propaganda

Goebbels (see page 42 for details of his biography) used his Ministry of Public Propaganda and Enlightenment and the Reich Chamber of Culture to control the thoughts, beliefs and opinions of the German people. Musicians, writers and actors had to be members of the Chamber.

It was important for the long-term future of the Third Reich that the majority of the population believed in the ideals of the Nazi Party. All aspects of the media were censored and skilfully manipulated by Goebbels. He used a variety of methods to ensure that even the fine arts, music, theatre and literature were controlled.

Newspapers

Non-Nazi newspapers and magazines were closed down. By 1935, the Nazis had closed down more than 1,600 newspapers and thousands of magazines. The Reich Press Law was passed in October 1933 and it resulted in the removal of Jewish and left-wing journalists. Editors were told by the Propaganda Ministry what could be printed and any foreign news which was published had to be taken from the Nazi-controlled German Press Agency.

Rallies

An annual mass rally was held at Nuremberg to advertise the power of the Nazi state and spectacular parades were held on other special occasions, such as Hitler's birthday (20 April). Local rallies and marches were led by the SA and the Hitler Youth (see page 92). The Nuremberg rallies would last for several days and attracted almost one million people each year after the Nazis came to power.

> **Source Q Goebbels explaining the use of propaganda**
> The finest kind of propaganda does not reveal itself. The best propaganda is that which works invisibly, penetrating every cell of life in such a way that the public has no idea of the aims of the propagandist.

> **Source S Orders from the Ministry of Propaganda, 1935**
> Photos showing members of the Reich government at dining tables in front of rows of bottles must not be published in the future. This has given the absurd impression that members of the government are living it up.

> **Practice question**
> Give two things you can infer from Source Q about Goebbels's use of propaganda. (For guidance, see page 78.)

> **ACTIVITIES**
> 1 Study Source S. Why do you think these orders were issued?
> 2 The following newspaper article has been given to you for censorship.
>   a) What will you remove or change?
>   b) Rewrite the article for publication.
>
> *Yesterday our tired-looking Führer, wearing his spectacles, met members of the Hitler Youth. However, only a small number turned up and our leader only had time to talk to one or two. He later attended a party to celebrate the anniversary of him becoming Chancellor. Lots of wine was consumed.*

▲ **Source R** A Nazi rally in northern Germany in the late 1930s

Radio

All radio stations were placed under Nazi control. Cheap mass-produced radios were sold and could be bought on instalments. By 1939, about 70 per cent of German families owned a radio. Sets were installed in cafés, factories, schools and offices and loudspeakers were placed in streets. It was important that the Nazi message was heard by as many people as possible, as much as was possible. Importantly, the People's Radio lacked shortwave reception, making it difficult for Germans to listen to foreign broadcasts.

Film

Goebbels also realised the popularity of the cinema, with over 100 films made each year and audiences exceeding 250 million in 1933. He was one of the first to realise its potential for propaganda. All film plots were shown to Goebbels before going into production. He realised that many Germans were bored by overtly political films. Instead love stories and thrillers were given pro-Nazi slants. One of the best known was *Hitlerjunge Quex* (1933), which tells the story of a boy who broke away from a Communist family to join the Hitler Youth, only to be murdered by Communists. All film performances were accompanied by a 45-minute official newsreel which glorified Hitler and Germany and publicised Nazi achievements.

One Nazi film director who gained international praise was Leni Riefenstahl. She produced a documentary called *Triumph of the Will* about the Nazi Party Conference and Rally of 1934 and also one about the 1936 Berlin Olympics.

Hitler ordered Goebbels to make anti-Semitic films but these were not always popular with audiences. However, they were made frequently after 1940.

Posters

Posters were cleverly used to put across the Nazi message, with the young particularly targeted. They were to be seen everywhere and the messages they contained were simple and direct.

▲ **Source U** A propaganda poster of 1934 which says 'Loyalty, Honour and Order'

Literature

All books, plays and poems were carefully censored and controlled to put across the Nazi message. Encouraged by Goebbels, students in Berlin burnt 20,000 books written by Jews, communists, and anti-Nazi university professors in a massive bonfire in Berlin in May 1933. There were similar burnings in other cities across Germany that year. Many writers were persuaded or forced to write books, plays and poems which praised Hitler's achievements. Some famous German writers such as the novelist Thomas Mann and poet and playwright Bertolt Brecht went into self-imposed exile rather than live under the Nazis. About 2,500 writers left Germany in the years up to 1939.

▲ **Source V** Students and members of the SA burning books in Berlin in May 1933

ACTIVITY

Make a copy of the following table. Use the sources and information on pages 73–75 to decide how effective each method of propaganda or censorship would have been. Add evidence to your table, one example has been done for you. Which would have had the greatest effect? Explain your choice.

	Very effective	Effective	Quite effective	Not effective
Radio	Available to most homes – 70% families by 1939			
Newspapers				
Cinema				
Posters				
Literature				
Rallies				

8.5 The Nazi control of the Arts

Just as it was important to control the media, Hitler realised that other aspects of everyday life could be controlled in order to re-inforce the ideology of Nazism. Thus, the Arts were controlled and people became used to seeing Nazi imagery in paintings, buildings and plays. It became impossible to avoid the message of the Nazis.

Music and theatre

Hitler hated modern music. Jazz, which was 'black' music, was seen as racially inferior and banned. Instead the Nazis encouraged traditional German folk music together with the classical music of Brahms, Beethoven and especially Richard Wagner, who was Hitler's favourite composer.

Theatre was to concentrate on German history and political drama. Cheap theatre tickets were available to encourage people to see plays, often with a Nazi political or racial theme.

Art and architecture

Hitler had earned a living as an artist and believed he was an expert in this area. He hated modern art (any art developed under the Weimar Republic), which he believed was backward, unpatriotic and Jewish. Such art was called 'degenerate'. This was banned. In its place, he encouraged art which highlighted Germany's past greatness and the strength and power of the Third Reich. He wanted art to reject the weak and ugly, and to glorify healthy, strong heroes. Artists were expected to portray workers, peasants and women as glorious and noble creatures. After 1934, it was decided that all new public buildings had to have sculptures which demonstrated Nazi ideals.

Hitler took a particular interest in architecture. He encouraged the 'monumental style' for public buildings. These were large buildings made of stone which were often copied from ancient Greece or Rome and showed the power of the Third Reich. Hitler admired the Greek and Roman styles of building because he said the Jews had not 'contaminated' it.

Paintings showed:

- the Nazi idea of the simple peasant life
- hard work as heroic
- the perfect Aryan; young German men and women were shown to have perfect bodies
- women in their preferred role as housewives and mothers.

ACTIVITIES

1 What message is the artist trying to put across in Source W?
2 You are a visitor to Nazi Germany. Explain how you came across Nazi ideas and views during one day of your stay.

◄ **Source W** *The Family*. This was painted in 1938 by a Nazi artist, Walter Willrich

8.6 The Nazi control of sport

Sport was encouraged at school and in the Hitler Youth. Hitler wanted a healthy and fit nation – the boys were to be the soldiers of the future and the girls were to produce as many children as possible. Success in sport was also important to promote the Nazi regime.

The major sporting showcase was the 1936 Olympics, which was staged in Berlin. Everything about the games was designed to impress the outside world (see Figure 8.4). With the media of 49 countries there in strength, the Nazis could show the world that Germany was a modern, well-organised society and that Aryans were superior. For the most part the Olympics was a great public relations success.

Source X From a speech by Goebbels, 23 April 1933

German sport has only one task: to strengthen the character of the German people, filling it with the fighting spirit and steadfast camaraderie necessary in the struggle for its existence.

The Olympic stadium was the largest in the world and could hold 110,000 spectators.

Signs declaring 'Jews not wanted' were removed. Foreign visitors got a positive image of Germany.

Every detail was carefully stage-managed and news reports were controlled.

Germany won more medals than any other nation – 33 gold, 26 silver and 30 bronze.

All filming was under the direction of Leni Riefenstahl. All camera crews had to be approved by her and all shots supervised.

▲ Figure 8.4 Summary of the 1936 Olympics

Source Y The Reich Youth Leader, Baldur von Schirach, explains what Hitler said to him after Jesse Owens' 100 metres victory

The Americans should be ashamed of themselves, letting Negroes win their medals for them. I shall not shake hands with this Negro. Do you really think that I will allow myself to be shaking hands with a Negro?

CASE STUDY: JESSE OWENS

The Berlin Olympics was meant to highlight the superiority of the Aryan race through the success of the German athletes. Hitler's plans were sabotaged by the success of the black athletes in the US Olympic team, especially Jesse Owens. Owens won the 100 metres, 200 metres, long jump and the 4 x 100 metres relay. He broke eleven Olympic records and was very popular with the German crowd. There were nine other black US athletes in the track and field events. Between them, they won seven gold medals. Hitler was not amused! He refused to present medals to the black athletes.

Practice question

Explain why sport changed under the Nazis in the years 1933–39.

You may use the following in your answer:
■ Healthy nation
■ Racial beliefs

You must also use information of your own.

(For further guidance, see pages 94–95.)

ACTIVITIES

1 Study Source Y. What was Hitler's attitude to Jesse Owens?
2 Imagine mobile phones existed in 1936. You witness Owens' victories and Hitler's reactions. Put together a text of the events to send to a friend. You may use text language. Maximum 160 characters.

8.7 Inference question

This section provides guidance on how to answer the source inference question.

Question 1

Give two things you can infer from Source A about the Catholic Church in Nazi Germany. (4 marks)

> **Source A** From police reports in Bavaria in 1937 and 1938
>
> The influence of the Catholic Church on the population is so strong that the Nazi spirit cannot penetrate. The local population is ever under the strong influence of the priests. These people prefer to believe what the priests say from the pulpit than the words of the best Nazi speakers.

How to answer

- You are being asked to give the message or messages of the source, to read between the lines of what is written.
- In addition, you must support the inference. In other words, use details from the source to support the messages you say it gives.
- Begin your answer with 'This source suggests...' This should help you get messages from the source.
- Aim for two supported inferences to be sure of full marks. For example, in Source A two messages could be:

Question 2

Give two things you can infer from Source B about the Gestapo. (4 marks)

> **Source B** From *Germany Reborn* by Hermann Goering, written in 1934 explaining his role in setting up the Gestapo
>
> Finally, I alone created, on my own initiative, the State Secret Police Department. This is the instrument which is so much feared by the enemies of the State, and which is chiefly responsible for the fact that in Germany and Prussia today there is no question of a Marxist or Communist danger.

ACTIVITY

Now have a go answering Question 2 using the steps shown for Question 1.

Inference
Source A suggests that the Nazis were not successful in controlling the Catholic Church.

Support from the source
I know this because the source says that the influence of the Catholic Church on the population is so strong that the Nazi spirit cannot penetrate.

Source A
The influence of the Catholic Church on the population is so strong that the Nazi spirit cannot penetrate. The local population is ever under the strong influence of the priests. These people prefer to believe what the priests say from the pulpit than the words of the best Nazi speakers.

Inference
Source A suggests that the German Catholics were controlled by their local priests.

Support from the source
I know this because the source says that the local population is ever under the strong influence of the priests.

9 Opposition, resistance and conformity in Nazi Germany

It was not easy to oppose the Nazi regime. From the beginning the Nazis were able to restrict challenges to their power by means of *Gleichschaltung* (see pages 57), the use of the Gestapo, SS and SD (see pages 65–67) and laws such as the banning of political parties and trade unions (see page 57). Many Germans knew that if they did object to the regime then it was probable that they would lose their jobs, and thus they silently accepted the Nazis. There was some opposition to the Hitler and the Nazi regime but it was never co-ordinated or unified. The young, the Church and the army did present some challenges to Hitler but they were never enough to threaten the regime in the years 1933 to 1939.

9.1 The extent of support for the Nazi regime

In the years 1933–39, there were about 1.3 million people sent to concentration camps in Germany and this would seem to be an indication of quite widespread opposition to the regime. It has also been estimated that about 300,000 left Germany to live in other countries, giving another indication of dissatisfaction with the Nazis.

Nevertheless, many Germans gained much from Hitler's successes after 1933 and consequently Hitler was readily able to maintain support. There were economic successes which began to erase the Depression. Germany's international standing grew and this seemed to remove the shame of defeat in the war and the Treaty of Versailles (the Saar was returned in 1935, the army was built up after 1935, and in 1936 the Rhineland was reoccupied). Some Germans were happy to see the Communists, Socialists and SA leaders removed.

Source A From a report of 1937 by the German Socialist Party in exile (SOPADE)

It becomes increasingly clear that the majority of the people have two faces; one which they show to their good and reliable acquaintances; and the other for the authorities, the Party officers, keen Nazis and for strangers. The private face shows the sharpest criticism of everything that is going on now; the official one shows optimism and contentment.

The army

In 1938, Hitler removed certain generals who had criticised his foreign policy aims – the most significant of whom were Blomberg, Fritsch and von Brauchitsch. During late 1938, some army leaders planned to overthrow Hitler but following his successful takeover of parts of Czechoslovakia, the plan was set aside.

In all, during 1938, Hitler removed 16 generals and thus tightened his grip on the army.

Assassination attempts

There were three attempts to assassinate Hitler before 1939. A number of Jewish students plotted in 1935–36 but the plans came to nothing. Maurice Bavaud, a student, tried to shoot Hitler at the annual Nazi parade in Munich but failed to take a shot because he did not want to injure other Nazi leaders. In November 1939, Georg Elser planted a bomb in the Beer Hall (where the 1923 Putsch had started – see page 33) where Hitler was speaking, but Hitler left early. The bomb exploded and killed several people. Elser despised the Nazi regime because it had taken basic liberties from ordinary people.

ACTIVITIES

1 What does Source A show about Nazi Germany?
2 Explain why was it important for Hitler to maintain control of the army.
3 Explain why opposition to the Nazis was so limited.

9.2 Opposition from young people to the Nazis

Although many of the young joined the Hitler Youth (see page 92), it was not popular with some of its members and not all young people accepted the Nazi ideas. Indeed by the mid-1930s gangs began to appear on street corners. They played their own music and boys and girls were free to be together. Many grew their hair long and wore their own choice of clothes as a rebellion against the regimentation of Nazi ideas. Some went looking for members of the Hitler Youth and beat them up.

> **Source B From a British magazine, 1938**
>
> There seems little enthusiasm for the Hitler Youth, with membership falling. Many no longer want to be commanded, but wish to do as they like. Usually only a third of a group appears for roll-call. At evening meetings it is a great event if 20 turn up out of 80, but usually there are only about 10 or 12.

> **Source C Hitler Youth member, private letter, 1936**
>
> How did we live in Camp S—, which is supposed to be an example to all the camps? We practically didn't have a minute of the day to ourselves. This isn't camp life, no sir! It's military barrack life! Drill starts right after a meagre breakfast. We would like to have athletics but there isn't any. Instead we have military exercises, down in the mud, till the tongue hangs out of your mouth. And we have only one wish: sleep, sleep …

> **Source D From the memoirs, written in the 1960s, of a German who was a student in the 1930s**
>
> No one in our class ever read *Mein Kampf*. I myself only used the book for quotations. In general we didn't do much about Nazi ideas. **Anti-Semitism** wasn't mentioned much by our teachers except through Richard Wagner's essay 'The Jews in Music'. We did, however, do a lot of physical education and cookery.

The Edelweiss Pirates

One such group was the Edelweiss Pirates. They listened to forbidden swing music and daubed walls with anti-Nazi graffiti. They could be recognised by their badges, for example the edelweiss flower or skull and crossbones. They wore clothes which were considered outlandish by the Nazis – check shirts, dark short trousers and white socks (see Source F). The earliest recorded groups were in 1934 and by 1939 they had a membership of 2,000. They were not a specific unified group but simply a loose band across many cities. In Cologne, they were called the Navajos, Düsseldorf had the Kittelbach Pirates and Essen had the Roving Dudes. The Pirates tended to be working-class youths. They created no-go areas for the Hitler Youth in their cities. Despite their activities, the Nazi authorities did not consider the Pirates to be a serious threat in the years to 1939.

Practice questions

1 How useful are Sources B and C for an enquiry into the Hitler Youth? Explain your answer, using Sources B and C and your knowledge of the historical context. (*For guidance, see pages 62–64.*)
2 Give two things you can infer from Source C about the Hitler Youth. (*For further guidance, see page 78.*)

Source E Verse from an Edelweiss Pirates' Song

Hitler's power may lay us low,
And keep us locked in chains,
But we will smash the chains one day.
We'll be free again.
We've got fists and we can fight.
We've got knives and we'll get them out.
We want freedom don't we boys?
We're the fighting Navajos.

The Swing Youth

Other young people who challenged the Nazis became known as the 'swing groups' and tended to come from the middle classes. They took part in activities that were frowned on by the Nazis. These young people loved swing music, which was hated by the Nazi government who classed it as non-German and as developed by black people and Jews. They rebelled against the order and discipline of the Nazis. Swing boys often grew their hair long and the girls wore make-up, using bright colours on their lips and fingernails.

▲ **Source F** Members of the Edelweiss Pirates, 1938

ACTIVITIES ?

1 In what ways does Source D challenge the accepted view of life in Nazi Germany?

2 Using Sources E and F, explain why you think some teenagers rebelled against the Hitler Youth.

3 Suggest reasons why the Nazis did not feel threatened by youth opposition in the years 1933–39.

4 Write a song or poem ancouraging young people to resist the Nazis.

▶ **Source G** German swing youth in 1930. The culture continued from 1930 and the methods of dress became more extreme through the Nazi era and into the war years

9.3 Opposition from the Churches

The Protestant Church

Pastor Martin Niemöller opposed Nazi control of the Church and became leader of the Confessional Church, which followed traditional German Protestantism. He established the Pastors' Emergency League, which opposed Nazi attempts to control the Protestant Church and saw membership rise to 7,000 by 1934. However, many pastors left when they were persecuted by the Nazis. Niemöller was arrested in 1937 after having preached that people must obey God and not man. He was tried and kept in prison and concentration camps until 1945.

Another protestant to speak out against Nazi ideas on religion was Agnes von Grone. She led the Protestant Women's Bureau but the organisation was disbanded in 1936.

> **Source I** From a lecture given by Niemöller after the end of the Second World War
>
> First they came for the socialists, and I did not speak out – Because I was not a socialist.
>
> Then they came for the trade unionists, and I did not speak out –
> Because I was not a trade unionist.
>
> Then they came for the Jews, and I did not speak out – Because I was not a Jew.
>
> Then they came for me – and there was no one left to speak for me.

The Catholic Church

Despite the Concordat (see page 71) with the Catholic Church there was tension after 1933 because the Nazis censored the Catholic press and harassed some of the priests. In 1937, Pope Pius XI issued a special letter (called an encyclical) to Catholic priests in Germany. He attacked the Nazi system although he never named Hitler and the Nazis in his criticisms. The encyclical was called '*Mit brennender Sorge*' ('With burning anxiety'). Priests read the letter to their congregations, clearly showing they were trying to resist the Nazi attempts to control the Church. However, the Nazi reaction was to take an even firmer line and close Catholic groups and prevent Catholics from joining the Nazi Party. There was a fierce outcry when symbols such as the cross and the crucifix were removed from Catholic schools, and following the complaints the Nazis halted these removals. Once war broke out in 1939, the Nazis reintroduced the policy of removal.

> **ACTIVITIES** ?
>
> 1 Study Source I. What message is Pastor Niemöller putting over?
> 2 Suggest reasons why Pope Pius did not mention Hitler and the Nazis in '*Mit brennender Sorge*'.
> 3 Work in pairs. Suggest reasons why opposition from the Protestant and Catholic Churches was rather limited.

◄ **Source H** Pastor Martin Niemöller, 1937

Life in Nazi Germany, 1933–39

This key topic examines the period from Hitler's appointment as Chancellor in 1933 to the outbreak of the Second World War in 1939. It examines how the lives of German citizens were changed by Nazi policies and whether people were better off under the Nazis. It also considers the racial policies of the Nazis and looks at the persecution of Jews and other minority groups in Germany.

Each chapter within this key topic explains a key issue and examines important lines of enquiry, as outlined in the boxes below.

There will also be guidance on how to answer the causation question (pages 94–95).

CHAPTER 10 NAZI POLICIES TOWARDS WOMEN

- Nazi views on women and family.
- Nazi policies towards women including marriage and family, employment and appearance.

CHAPTER 11 NAZI POLICIES TOWARDS THE YOUNG

- Nazi aims and policies towards the young. The Hitler Youth and the League of German Maidens.
- Nazi control through education, including the curriculum and teachers.

CHAPTER 12 EMPLOYMENT AND LIVING STANDARDS

- Nazi policies to reduce unemployment including labour services, autobahns, rearmament and invisible unemployment.
- Changes in the standard of living, especially of German workers. The Labour Front, Strength through Joy, Beauty of Labour.

CHAPTER 13 THE PERSECUTION OF THE MINORITIES

- Nazi racial beliefs and policies and the treatment of minorities: Slavs, Gypsies, homosexuals and those with disabilities.
- The persecution of the Jews, including the boycott of Jewish shops and businesses (1933), the Nuremberg Laws and Kristallnacht.

TIMELINE

1933	Boycott of Jewish shops and businesses	1935	Conscription introduced
	Law for the Encouragement of Marriage passed	1936	Membership of the Hitler Youth made compulsory
	Sterilisation Law passed	1938	Jewish children were not allowed to attend German schools
	First concentration camp for women opened at Moringen		*Lebensborn* programme introduced
	First Napola schools set up		Kristallnacht
1935	The Nuremberg Laws passed (the Reich Citizenship Law and the Law to Protect German Blood and Honour)	1939	The euthanasia campaign began
			Designated Jewish ghettos established

10 Nazi policies towards women

Nazi policies towards women reflected Hitler's own personal views. He hated the changes in the position of women in society, which had occurred in the 1920s, and wanted to create a society where women had a precise and specific domestic role. He did not want women to be involved in the world of work and saw their task as bearing and rearing children while their husbands worked. Hitler believed that education for women should be focused on their future role in society and hence that it should prepare them for marriage and motherhood.

Though most women accepted the policies imposed by the Nazis, there were some who did not and were active in opposing the loss of their rights. These women were eventually arrested and sent to concentration camps.

10.1 The Nazi view of the role of women

Women had made significant progress in their position in German society during the 1920s, as the table below shows.

Political	Economic	Social
Women over 20 were given the vote and took an increasing interest in politics. By 1933 one-tenth of the members of the Reichstag were female.	Many women took up careers in the professions, especially the civil service, law, medicine and teaching. Those in the civil service earned the same as men. By 1933 there were 100,000 women teachers and 3,000 doctors.	Socially, women went out unescorted, drank and smoked in public, were fashion conscious, often wearing relatively short skirts, had their hair cut short and wore make-up.

Nazi policies

The Nazis brought in a series of measures to change the role of women. One of the first actions of the Nazis, as part of the *Gleichschaltung* process, was to bring all 230 women's organisations together under one body – the Women's Front (*Frauenfront*). The women's groups were then expected to ensure that Jews could not be members. In 1934, Getrude Scholtz-Klink was appointed National Women's Leader of Germany.

Nazi ideals

The Nazis had a very traditional view of the role of women, which was very different from women's position in society in the 1920s. According to the Nazi ideal, a woman:

- did not wear make-up
- was blonde, heavy hipped and athletic
- wore flat shoes and a full skirt
- did not smoke
- did not go out to work
- did all the household duties, especially cooking and bringing up the children
- took no interest in politics.

Source A Goebbels describes the role of women in 1929

The mission of women is to be beautiful and to bring children into the world. The female bird pretties herself for her mate and hatches eggs for him. In exchange, the male takes care of gathering the food and stands guard and wards off the enemy.

Source B From a speech by Gertrude Scholtz-Klink, after she became Head of the Nazi Women's Organisation in 1933

Woman is entrusted in the life of the nation with a great task, the care of man – soul, body and mind. It is the mission of woman to minister in the home and in her profession to the needs of life from the first to the last moment of man's existence. Her mission is comrade, helper, and womanly complement of man – this the right of woman in the new Germany.

Source C A German rhyme addressed to women

Take hold of the kettle, broom and pan,
Then you'll surely get a man!
Shop and office leave alone,
Your true life work lies at home.

ACTIVITIES

1 What, according to Source A, was the role of women in Nazi Germany?

2 Does Source B support Source A about the Nazi view of the role of women?

3 Draw sketches of two women.
   a) Label the first sketch with the features of a 'modern woman' during the 1920s.
   b) Label the second with the Nazi view of women.

4 You are an Edelweiss Pirate. Write a four-line poem rejecting Source C.

5 What is the message of Source D in relation to the role of women in Nazi society?

Practice question

Give two things you can infer from Source B about the role of women in Nazi Germany.
(*For further guidance, see page 78.*)

▼ **Source D** A painting completed in 1939 by Adolf Wissel, entitled *Farm Family from Kahlenberg*

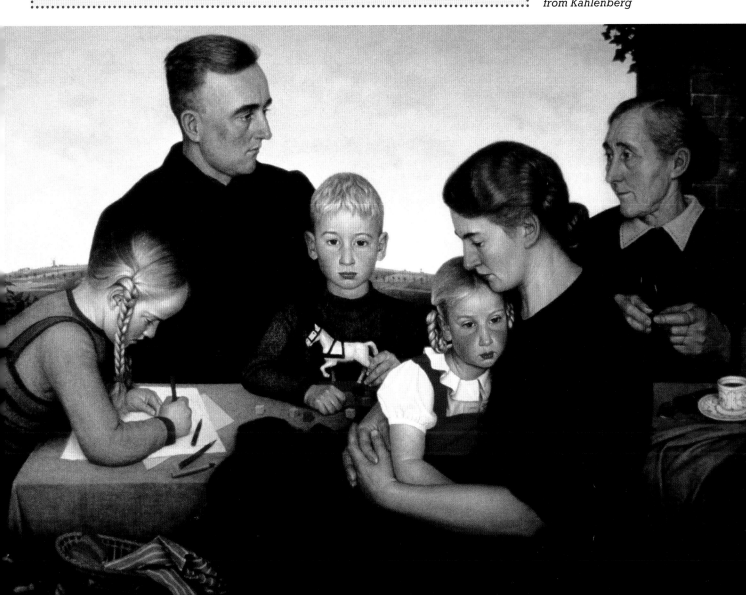

10.2 The changing role of women

Marriage and family

The Nazis were very worried by the decline in the birth rate. In 1900 there had been over 2 million live births per year but this had dropped to under 1 million in 1933. The number of live births rose to 1.4 million in 1939 and though Jews were allowed to have abortions, non-Jews were not.

- A massive propaganda campaign was launched to promote motherhood and large families.
- In 1933 the Law for the Encouragement of Marriage was introduced. This aimed to increase Germany's falling birth-rate by giving loans to help young couples to marry, provided the wife left her job. Couples were allowed to keep one quarter of the loan for each child born up to four.
- On Hitler's mother's birthday (12 August) medals were awarded to women with large families (see Figure 10.1).
- Family allowances were made available to those on low incomes.
- In 1938 the Nazis changed the divorce law – a divorce was possible if a husband or wife could not have children. This contributed to an increase in the divorce rate by 1939.
- The Nazis also set up the *Lebensborn* ('fount of life') programme whereby specially chosen unmarried women could 'donate a baby to the Führer' by becoming pregnant by 'racially pure' SS men.
- A new national organisation, the German Women's Enterprise, organised classes and radio talks on household topics and the skills of motherhood.
- University enrolment for women was limited to 10 per cent of the total entry.
- The Sterilisation Law (1933) (see Source E) resulted in 320,000 being sterilised due to 'mental deficiency'.
- The Marriage Health Law of 1935 (see Source F) stressed the racial purity of women when marrying.

> **Source E** From the Law for the Prevention of Genetically Diseased Offspring, 1933 (the Sterilisation Law)
>
> Anyone who has a hereditary illness can be rendered sterile by a surgical operation if, according to the experience of medical science, there is a strong probability that his or her offspring will suffer from serious hereditary defects of a physical or mental nature.

> **Source F** From Outlines of Law for the Protection of the Hereditary Health of the German People, 1935 (Marriage Health Law)
>
> Remember you are a German.
> Remain pure in mind and spirit!
> Keep your body pure!
> If hereditarily fit, do not remain single!
> Marry only for love.
> Being a German, only choose a spouse of similar or related blood!
> When choosing your spouse, inquire into his forebears!
> Health is essential to outward beauty as well!
> Seek a companion in marriage, not a playmate.
> Hope for as many children as possible! Your duty is to produce at least four offspring in order to ensure the future of the national stock.

▲ Figure 10.1 The Cross of Honour of the German Mother was awarded in bronze (four to five children), silver (six to seven children) and gold (eight or more)

▲ **Source G** German cartoon from the 1930s. The caption reads 'Introducing Frau Müller who up to now has brought 12 children into the world'

ACTIVITIES

1 Study Source E. Explain why this law was passed.

2 In what ways does Source F show the Nazis' real attitude towards women?

3 What message is the cartoonist trying to put across in Source G?

4 Explain why Source H was published in Nazi newspapers across Germany.

Nazi organisations for women

Table 10.1 shows the key organisations for women in Nazi Germany. Once more, the Nazis ensured that the lives of all sections of society were controlled.

▼ Table 10.1 Nazi organisations for women and girls

Age	Organisations
10–14	*Jungmädelbund* (Young Girls League)
14–18	*Bund Deutscher Mädel* (League of German Maidens)
18–21	*Glaube und Schönheit* (Faith and Beauty Society)
+21	Women's Front (*Frauenfront*)
+21	Reich Mothers' Service (this trained midwives and housewives)

▲ **Source H** Members of the League of German Maidens going on a hike in 1936

Appearance

Women were encouraged to keep healthy and wear their hair in a bun or plaits. They were discouraged from wearing trousers, high heels and make-up, dyeing or styling their hair and slimming, as this was seen as bad for childbearing.

> **Source I** Marianne Gartner was a member of the League of German Girls and remembers one of its meetings in 1936
>
> At one meeting the team leader raised her voice. 'There is no greater honour for a German woman than to bear children for the Führer and for the Fatherland! The Führer has ruled that no family will be complete without at least four children. A German woman does not use make-up! A German woman does not smoke! She has a duty to keep herself fit and healthy! Any questions?' 'Why isn't the Führer married and a father himself?' I asked.

Work

Instead of going to work, women were asked to follow the 'three Ks' – *Kinder, Küche, Kirche* – 'children, kitchen, church'. The Nazis had another incentive to get women to give up work. They had been elected partly because they promised more jobs. Every job left by a woman was available for a man.

Women doctors, civil servants and teachers were forced to leave their jobs. After 1936, women could not become judges nor could they serve on juries. Schoolgirls were trained for work at home (see page 91). They were discouraged from going on to higher education.

However, from 1937, the Nazis had to reverse these policies. Germany began to rearm and men were joining the army. The Nazi regime therefore needed more women to go out to work. They abolished the marriage loans and introduced a compulsory 'duty year' for all women entering employment. This usually meant helping on a farm or in a family home in return for bed and board but no pay. The number of women working increased from 11.6 million in 1933 to 14.6 million in 1939 (see Figure 10.2).

▲ **Source J** Members of the League of German Maidens would babysit while the mothers were at work

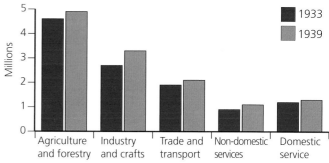

▲ Figure 10.2 Employment of women

Concentration camps

Many German women did not agree with the ideas and policies of the Nazis. In October 1933, the Nazis opened the first concentration camp for women at Moringen. Those sent to Moringen included communists, Jehovah's Witnesses, breakers of the Nuremberg Laws (see page 107), abortionists, those who had made derogatory remarks about the Nazi regime, and Jews. Ravensbrück camp was opened in 1939 to take the Moringen prisoners. By the end of 1939, there were more than two thousand prisoners at Ravensbrück and this included some 400 Gypsies.

▲ **Source K** Women prisoners at Ravensbrück concentration camp, 1939

ACTIVITIES

1 What can you learn from Source J about the role of women in Nazi Germany?
2 Why might Source I have been censored by the Nazis?

Practice question

How useful are Sources G (page 86) and I for an enquiry into the life for women in Nazi Germany? Explain your answer, using Sources G and I and your knowledge of the historical context. (*For guidance, see pages 62–64.*)

Were these policies successful?

By looking carefully at the sources below and answering the activity questions you will be able to make your own mind up whether Nazi policies towards women had any success.

Source L Extract from a letter from several women to a Leipzig newspaper in 1934

Today man is educated not for, but against, marriage. We see our daughters growing up in stupid aimlessness living only in a vague hope of getting a man and having children. A son, even the youngest, laughs in his mother's face. He regards her as his servant and women in general are merely willing tools of his aims.

Source M Toni Christen, an American journalist writing in 1939

I talked to Mrs Schmidt, a woman of about 50, as she came out of the shop. 'You see, older women are no good in Germany,' she said. 'We are no longer capable of bearing children. We have no value to the state. They don't care for us mothers or grandmothers any more. We are worn out, discarded.'

Source N Judith Grunfeld, an American journalist, 1937

How many women workers did the Führer send home? According to the statistics of the German Department of Labour, there were in June 1936, 5,470,000 employed women, or 1,200,000 more than in January 1933. The Nazi campaign has not been successful in reducing the numbers of women employed. It has simply squeezed them out of better paid positions into the sweated trades. This type of labour with its miserable wages and long hours is extremely dangerous to the health of women and degrades the family.

Source O The views of Wilhelmine Haferkamp, who was 22 in 1933. She lived in the industrial city of Oberhausen

When one had ten children, well not ten but a pile of them, one had to join the Nazi Party. 1933 it was and I already had three children and the fourth on the way. When 'child-rich' people were in the Party the children had a great chance to advance. I got 30 marks per child from the Hitler government and 20 marks per child from the city. That was a lot of money. I sometimes got more 'child money' than my husband earned.

ACTIVITIES

1   Make a copy of the following table. Sort Sources L–O into successes and failures for Nazi policies in the areas of marriage and family and jobs. Complete the grid with an explanation of your choices. One has been done for you.

	Success	Failure
Marriage and family		Source M as the Nazis did not value older women
Jobs		

2   You are a British journalist who has visited Nazi Germany in 1938 to investigate the role of women. Use the work you have done in Activity 1 to write an article explaining the successes and failures of Nazi policies. You will need a catchy headline. You could include imaginary interviews.

11 Nazi policies towards the young

Hitler saw the young as the future of the Third Reich. He spoke of the Thousand Year Reich and this would not be achieved unless the youth of Germany was converted to the Nazi way of thinking. Young people had to be converted to Nazi ideals such as obedience, following the Führer, placing the nation first, strengthening the racial purity of the nation and having large numbers of children. These aims were to be achieved through control of education and the Hitler Youth. If young people were indoctrinated at school and then in their leisure time, they would become loyal and committed followers of Hitler and would not want to criticise the Nazi way of life.

11.1 Control of the young through education

When the Nazis came to power, they established the Ministry for Science, Education and National Culture with Bernhard Rust at its head. Before 1933, the regional *Länder* (see page 57) had been responsible for education, now it was the government's responsibility.

Everyone in Germany had to go to school from the age of six until the age of fourteen. After that, schooling was optional. Boys and girls went to separate schools. In 1938, Jewish children were not allowed to attend German schools. Restrictions were placed on Jews going to university and many Jewish lecturers were not allowed to teach. Figure 11.1 shows the extent and breadth of Nazi control in schools after 1933.

Schools

At school academic ability was not the most important feature – the Nazis sought courage and prowess in athletics. The Nazis set up their own types of schools, which were designed for those who would be the future leaders of the state. National Political Training Institutes (*Nationalpolitische Lehranstalt* – 'Napola') took boys from the age of 10 up to 18 and on graduation many went into the armed forces or the Nazi paramilitary groups. The SS (see page 66) took control of the Napola schools after 1936.

Adolf Hitler Schools were for students between the ages of 12 and 18 and were mainly for the elite of the Hitler Youth.

Ordensburgen ('order castles') were for graduates of the Adolf Hitler Schools and entrants were usually in their 20s. Live ammunition was used in war games and there were instances of students being killed during these activities.

> **Source A** Robert Ley, leader of the German Labour Front
>
> We start our work when the child is three. As soon as it begins to think, a little flag is put in its hand. Then comes school, the Hitler Youth movement, the storm troopers. We never let a single soul go, and when they have gone through all that, there is the labour front (DAF), which takes them when they are grown up and never lets go of them, whether they like it or not.

ACTIVITIES

1 What does Source A show about the intention of Ley and the Nazis towards children and young people?
2 Study Source B. Why do you think the Nazi-controlled schools used this question?
3 Choose a subject in the curriculum. Devise a question or problem that would reflect Nazi ideals with regard to: hatred of communism, the desire to destroy the Treaty of Versailles, and the desire to make Germany great.

TEXTBOOKS

These were rewritten to fit the Nazi view of history and racial purity. All textbooks had to be approved by the Ministry of Education. *Mein Kampf* became a standard text.

TEACHERS

School teachers had to swear an oath of loyalty to Hitler and join the **Nazi Teachers' League**. By 1937, 97 per cent of teachers had joined. Teachers had to promote Nazi ideals in the classroom and many were dismissed if they did not show that they were committed to Nazism. By 1936, 36 per cent of teachers were members of the Nazi Party.

LESSONS

These began and ended with the students saluting and saying *'Heil Hitler'*. Nazi themes were presented through every subject. Maths problems dealt with social issues. Geography lessons were used to show how Germany was surrounded by hostile neighbours. In history lessons, students were taught about the evils of communism and the severity of the Treaty of Versailles.

CURRICULUM

Under the Nazis the school curriculum was changed to prepare students for their future roles. Hitler wanted healthy, fit men and women so 15 per cent of time was devoted to physical education. With the boys the emphasis was on preparation for the military. There was also great emphasis on Germany's past and the **Aryan** race. Students were taught that Aryans were superior and should not marry inferior races such as Jews. Girls took needlework and home crafts, especially cookery, to become good homemakers and mothers. New subjects such as race studies were introduced to put across Nazi ideas on race and population control. Children were taught how to measure their skulls and to classify racial types. Religious education became optional.

▲ Figure 11.1 How Nazis controlled schools after 1933

Source B A question from a maths textbook, 1933

The Jews are aliens in Germany. In 1933 there were 66,060,000 inhabitants of the German **Reich**, of whom 499,862 were Jews. What is the percentage of aliens in Germany?

Source C From the memoirs, written in the 1960s, of a German who was a student in the 1930s

No one in our class ever read *Mein Kampf*. I myself only used the book for quotations. In general we didn't do much about Nazi ideas. **Anti-Semitism** wasn't mentioned much by our teachers except through Richard Wagner's essay 'The Jews in Music'. We did, however, do a lot of physical education and cookery.

▲ **Source D** A teacher with her students during a history lesson, *c.* 1933

Practice question

Give two things you can infer from Source C about education in Nazi Germany. (*For guidance, see page 78.*)

11.2 The Hitler Youth

The Nazis also wanted to control the young in their spare time. This was to be achieved through the Hitler Youth, which covered both boys and girls. The head of the Hitler Youth was Baldur von Schirach.

- All other youth organisations were banned.
- From 1936 membership was compulsory, though many did not join.
- By 1939 there were seven million members. Many enjoyed the comradeship. It is also possible they enjoyed the fact that their camps were often near to those of the League of German Maidens.

▼ Table 11.1 Nazi boys' organisations

Name of group	Age	Activities
Little Fellows (*Pimpfe*)	6–10	Sport, hiking, camping
German Young People (*Deutsches Jungvolk*)	10–13	Military preparation
Hitler Youth (*Hitlerjugend*)	14–18	Training for the military

▼ Table 11.2 Nazi girls' organisations. To join, girls had to be of German heritage, a German citizen and free of hereditary diseases

Name of group	Age	Activities
Young Girls' League (*Jungmädelbund*)	10–14	Sport, camping
League of German Maidens (*Bund Deutscher Mädel*)	14–18	Lessons in preparation for motherhood, a compulsory year working on the land, domestic science, physical exercise, parades and marches.
Faith and Beauty (*Glaube und Schönheit*)	18–21 (voluntary membership)	Continued training for marriage and life as a housewife. Classes on clothes making and cooking healthy meals.

ACTIVITY ?

You have been asked by your local Hitler Youth to produce a poster promoting the organisation. You could use either Source E or F as the illustration for your poster and get more ideas from Source E.

▲ **Source E** A recruiting poster for the Hitler Youth, 1933, which says in the poster 'Come to us!' and at the foot: 'Join the Hitler Youth'

▲ **Source F** A recruiting poster for the Young Girls' League which says 'Every ten year old to us'

How successful were these policies?

Although many of the young people who joined the Hitler Youth enjoyed it, it was not popular with some of its members.

Source G The memories of a Hitler Youth leader

What I liked about the Hitler Youth was the comradeship. I was full of enthusiasm when I joined the Young People at the age of ten. I can still remember how deeply moved I was when I heard the club mottoes: 'Young People are hard. They can keep a secret. They are loyal. They are comrades.' And then there were the trips! Is anything nicer than enjoying the splendours of the homeland in the company of one's comrades?

Source H From a British magazine, 1938

There seems little enthusiasm for the Hitler Youth, with membership falling. Many no longer want to be commanded, but wish to do as they like. Usually only a third of a group appears for roll-call. At evening meetings it is a great event if 20 turn up out of 80, but usually there are only about 10 or 12.

Source I Hitler Youth member, private letter, 1936

How did we live in Camp S—, which is supposed to be an example to all the camps? We practically didn't have a minute of the day to ourselves. This isn't camp life, no sir! It's military barrack life! Drill starts right after a meagre breakfast. We would like to have athletics but there isn't any. Instead we have military exercises, down in the mud, till the tongue hangs out of your mouth. And we have only one wish: sleep, sleep...

▼ Source J Members of the League of German Maidens going on a hike, 1937

11.5 Causation question

This section provides guidance on how to answer the causation question. Look at the question below:

Question 1

Explain why there were changes to the lives of young people in Nazi Germany in the years 1933–39.

> You may use the following in your answer:
> - Nazi ideals
> - Education
>
> You **must** also use information of your own.

How to answer

- Ensure you do not simply describe the two given points.
- Focus on the key words in the question, for example the theme of the question, which is causation, and any dates.
- Make use of at least the two given points and one of your own, or develop at least three points of your own.
- Write an introduction that identifies the key areas you are going to explain in your answer.
- Write one good length paragraph on each point, fully explaining each.

The diagram on page 95 shows the steps you should take to write a good answer to this question. Use the steps and examples to complete an answer to the question by writing paragraphs on each point (your own and those given) and linking them where possible. Alternatively you could use the flowchart below to structure your answer to the question.

INTRODUCTION
- Explain the key theme of the question.
- Suggest the key areas you are going to cover in your answer.

FIRST PARAGRAPH – FIRST GIVEN REASON (OR REASON OF YOUR OWN)
- Introduce the first reason.
- Fully explain this reason.

SECOND PARAGRAPH – SECOND GIVEN REASON (OR REASON OF YOUR OWN)

THIRD PARAGRAPH – REASON OF YOUR OWN (OR GIVEN REASON IF NOT YET COVERED)

Step 1
Write an introduction that identifies the key reasons you need to cover in your answer and your main argument.

Example

In the years 1933-39 the life of young people changed considerably under the Nazis. This was due to a number of reasons including Nazi ideals about control of the young, education and the influence of the Hitler Youth.

Step 2
Write at least one good length paragraph for each of at least three reasons.
For each paragraph:
- Introduce the reason (green in the example).
- Fully explain it (blue in the example).

Example

The first reason for changes to the lives of young people in Nazi Germany in the years 1933-39 was Nazi ideals on the young. Hitler saw the young as the future of the Third Reich. Hitler spoke of the Thousand Year Reich and this would not be achieved unless the youth of Germany was converted to the Nazi way of thinking. Young people had to be converted to Nazi ideals such as obedience, following the Führer, placing the nation first, strengthening the racial purity of the nation and having a large number of children. This was important because these aims were to be achieved through control of education and the Hitler Youth. If young people were indoctrinated at school and then in their leisure time, they would become loyal and committed followers of Hitler and would not want to criticise the Nazi way of life.

Step 3
Now do the same for the second reason.

Example

A further reason for changes to the lives of young people in Nazi Germany in the years 1933-39 was control of the young through education.

Step 4
Complete this paragraph and write one more paragraph on another reason.

Question 2

Explain why the Hitler Youth had only mixed success among the young German people.

You may use the following in your answer:
- Comradeship
- Compulsory membership

You **must** also use information of your own.

ACTIVITY

Now have a go answering Question 2 using the steps shown for Question 1.

12 Employment and living standards

One of the main reasons for increased support for the Nazis was the high level of unemployment, which had reached six million by 1932. Hitler had promised that he would reduce and remove unemployment that had been caused by the Great Depression (see pages 39–40). Through a variety of methods, he kept his promise to achieve full employment. However, were workers better off under the Nazis?

12.1 Policies were introduced to reduce unemployment

Hitler introduced a series of measures to reduce unemployment.

The Reich Labour Service

This was a scheme to provide young men with manual labour jobs. From 1935 it was compulsory for all men aged 18–25 to serve in the corps for six months. Workers lived in camps, wore uniforms, received very low pay and carried out military drill as well as working (see Sources A and B).

Invisible unemployment

The Nazis used some dubious methods to keep down the unemployment figures. The official figures did not include the following:

- Jews dismissed from their jobs.
- Unmarried men under 25 who were pushed into National Labour schemes.
- Women dismissed from their jobs or who gave up work to get married.
- Opponents of the Nazis put in concentration camps.

The figures also included part-time workers as fully employed.

▼ Source B Young men in the Labour Service carrying out a military drill in 1933

Source A An Austrian visitor describes a Labour Service camp in 1938

The camps are organised on thoroughly military lines. The youths wear uniforms like soldiers. The only difference is that they carry spades instead of rifles and work in the fields.

Job creation schemes

Hitler at first spent billions on job creation schemes, rising from 18.4 billion marks in 1933 to 37.1 billion five years later. The Nazis subsidised private firms, especially in the construction industry. They also introduced a massive road-building programme to provide Germany with 7,000 kilometres of autobahns (motorways) (see Source C). However, only just over 3,000 kilometres had been built by 1938. More than 125,000 men were involved in their construction and Hitler hoped the autobahns would enable his troops to move rapidly in the event of war.

▲ **Source C** An official photograph showing workers gathering to begin work on the first autobahn, September 1933

THE ROAD TO FULL EMPLOYMENT

2,520,000 1936
1,853,000 1937
1,052,000 1938
302,000 1939

▼ **Source D** A photograph of German armed forces, 13 September 1937

Rearmament

Hitler was determined to build up the armed forces in readiness for war. This greatly reduced unemployment.

- The re-introduction of conscription in 1935 took thousands of young men into military service. The army grew from 100,000 in 1933 to 1,400,000 by 1939.
- Heavy industry expanded to meet the needs of rearmament. Coal and chemicals doubled in the years 1933 to 1939; oil, iron and steel trebled.
- Billions were spent producing tanks, aircraft and ships. In 1933, 3.5 billion marks was spent on rearmament. This had increased to 26 billion marks by 1939.

ACTIVITIES ?

1. What can you learn from Sources A and B about the Reich Labour Service? Explain your answer.
2. Why do you think Source C was taken?

Practice questions

1. How useful are Sources A and B for an enquiry into the Reich Labour Service? Explain your answer, using Sources A and B and your knowledge of the historical context. (*For guidance, see pages 62–64.*)
2. Explain why there was a great reduction in unemployment in Germany in the years 1933–39.

You may use the following in your answer:
- Rearmament
- The Reich Labour Service

You must also use information of your own.

(for guidance, see page2 94–95)

12.2 Changes in the standard of living

Better off

The Nazis were aware that compulsion alone could not fully guarantee complete obedience to the government. To win workers over and make them feel part of the creation of the people's community (*Volksgemeinschaft*) various schemes were introduced. These acted as incentives and they proved quite successful.

Strength through Joy (*Kraft durch Freude* – KdF)

This was an organisation set up by the German Labour Front (see page 57). The KdF tried to improve the leisure time of German workers by sponsoring a wide range of leisure and cultural trips. These included concerts, theatre visits, museum tours, sporting events, weekend trips, holidays and cruises. All were provided at a low cost, giving ordinary workers access to activities normally reserved for the better off. In 1938, more than 10 million people took KdF holidays.

> **Source E** Extract from the Strength through Joy magazine, 1936
>
> KdF is now running weekly theatre trips to Munich from the countryside. Special theatre trains are coming to Munich on weekdays from as far away as 120 kilometres. So a lot of our comrades who used to be in the Outdoor Club, for example, are availing themselves of the opportunity of going on trips with KdF. There is simply no other choice. Walking trips have also become very popular.

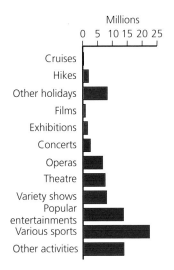

▲ Figure 12.1 Official numbers taking part in KdF activities in 1938

◀ **Source F** A Strength through Joy poster of 1938 encouraging German workers to go on cruises

ACTIVITY ❓

What can you learn from Sources E, F, G and Figure 12.1 about the KdF?

Beauty of Labour

This was a department of the KdF that tried to improve working conditions. It organised the building of canteens, swimming pools and sports facilities. It also installed better lighting in workplaces and improved noise levels.

Volkswagen scheme

In 1938 the Labour Front organised the Volkswagen ('people's car') scheme, giving workers an opportunity to subscribe five marks a week to a fund eventually allowing them to acquire a car.

Wages

Average weekly wages rose from 86 marks in 1932 to 109 marks in 1938.

Food consumption

As in every sphere of life, food became a target of Nazi propaganda. Women were informed which food to buy and how to cook simple meals which were healthy and cheap. The '*Eintopf*' (a one-pot dish comprising meat and vegetables) was encouraged and became known as the 'meal of sacrifice for the nation'.

▲ **Source G** German workers on a KdF cruise in 1935

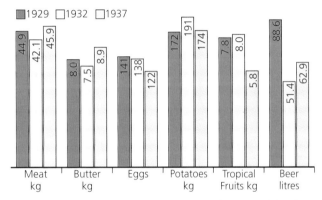

▲ Figure 12.2 Consumption per head of selected foods

Worse off

Although the Nazis offered schemes and incentives to workers, not all workers benefitted. Women were denied employment opportunities (see page 88), some basic rights of workers were removed and the cost of living rose.

Lack of freedom

German workers lost their rights under the Nazis. In 1933 trade unions were banned and they were replaced by the German Labour Front. The Labour Front was designed to have all workers and employers striving to create the *Volksgemeinschaft*. The Labour Front did not permit workers to negotiate for better pay or reduced hours of work and strikes were banned. Those who opposed the Nazis were rounded up and sent to concentration camps for re-education. The Reich Labour Service (*Reichsarbeitsdienst*, RAD) made six months' labour service compulsory for all men aged between the ages of 19 and 25.

Strength through Joy

Very few workers could actually afford the more expensive activities such as cruises to Madeira and Scandinavia. Beauty of Labour caused much resentment as workers had to carry out improvements in their spare time and without pay.

Volkswagen swindle

The idea to encourage people to save to buy a Volkswagen was a con trick. Despite being encouraged to put aside money every week, by the time war broke out in 1939 not a single customer had taken delivery of a car. None of the money was refunded.

Cost of living

The cost of living increased during the 1930s. All basic groceries, except fish, cost more in 1939 than they had in 1933. Food items were in short supply partly because it was government policy to reduce agricultural production. This was to keep up the prices for the benefit of the farmers. Source H is an indication of what how foreigners saw the issue of food consumption in Germany in 1934.

Hours of work

The average working hours in industry increased from 42.9 per week in 1933 to 47 in 1939. Sources I and J and Figure 12.3 give clear indications of the hard work and long hours workers were expected to perform under the Nazi regime.

▲ **Source H** A French cartoon of 1934. The caption reads 'What! Bread? Don't you know the Nazi revolution is over?'

Source I Report from the Social Democratic Party on labour service, 1938

The young people are deadened by physical exertion. They have to get up very early and have very little time to themselves. The whole aim of the service seems to be to pass on Nazi ideas and prepare them for military service. The pay is pitiful. Barely enough to buy a beer.

Source J From the memoirs of a German who experienced labour service, 1936

We started physical exercise at a ridiculously early time. Before and after work we got military drill and instruction. We worked outdoors in all kinds of weather for the sum of only 51 pfennigs an hour. Then they took off deductions and voluntary contributions, including 15 pfennigs for a straw mattress and draughty barracks and 35 pfennigs for what they ladle out of a cauldron and call dinner – slop – you wouldn't touch it, I guarantee it.

04.45	Get up.
04.50	Gymnastics.
05.15	Wash and make beds.
05.30	Coffee break.
05.50	Parade.
06.00	March to building site.
Work till 14.30 with 30 minute break for breakfast.	
15.00	Lunch.
15.30–18.00	Drill.
18.10–18.45	Instruction.
18.45–19.15	Cleaning and mending.
19.15	Parade.
19.30	Announcements.
19.45	Supper.
20.00–21.30	Sing-song or other leisure activities.
22.00	Lights out.

▲ Figure 12.3 The daily programme in a Labour Service camp in 1938

ACTIVITIES

1 Study Source H. What is the message of the cartoon?

2 Study Sources I and J. Do they support the view that Labour Service was unpopular?

3 Work in pairs. Imagine you interview a male German worker in 1938. You are trying to find out how his lifestyle has changed under the Nazis.
   ☐ Think of three questions you would ask him.
   ☐ Write down possible answers to the questions.

4 Make a copy of this pair of scales and write in evidence of German workers being better or worse off. Overall, what does your pair of scales reveal?

5 Explain how the position of German workers changed in the years 1933–39.

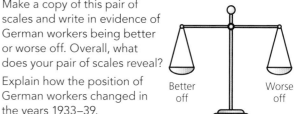
Better off   Worse off

13 The persecution of minorities

In order to win support in the years before 1933, Hitler had used the Jews as scapegoats for many of Germany's problems, including German defeat in the First World War and the harshness of the Treaty of Versailles. Once in power, the Nazi propaganda machine was used to turn more and more Germans against the Jews and justify a policy of persecution. Jews were not the only ones who did not fit Hitler's ideal of the 'pure' Aryan German, and during the 1930s many groups such as Gypsies, homosexual people and mentally and physically disabled people were targeted and persecuted. Action against the minority groups began in 1933 at a low level but by the end of the 1930s many in these groups had had property destroyed and were imprisoned in concentration camps.

13.1 Nazi racial beliefs

Central to Nazi policy was the creation of a pure German state. This meant treating all non-German groups, especially Jewish people, as second-class citizens. Hitler's theory of race was based on the idea of the 'master race' and the 'subhumans'. He tried to back up this theory by saying that the Bible showed there were only two races – the Jews and the Aryans – and that God had a special purpose for the Aryans. Hitler's view was that the Aryans would be a *Volksgemeinschaft* – a people's community – which would work for the good of Germany.

The Nazis believed that the Germans were a pure race of Aryan descent – from the *Herrenvolk* or 'master race'. They were shown in art as blond, blue-eyed, tall, lean and athletic – a people considered fit to master the world. However, this race had been contaminated by the subhumans.

Hitler believed that Germany's future was dependent on the creation of a pure Aryan racial state. This would be achieved by:

- selective breeding
- destroying the Jews.

Selective breeding meant preventing anyone who did not conform to the Aryan type from having children. The SS was part of the drive for selective breeding. It recruited men who were of Aryan blood, tall, fair-haired and blue-eyed. They were only allowed to marry women of Aryan blood. Mixed marriages or mixed relationships were not allowed (see Source A). Indeed, the Nazis even encouraged SS members and Aryan women to have children out of wedlock in order to further the *Herrenvolk*.

◀ **Source A** A non-Jewish wife and her Jewish husband being humiliated by SA troops in 1938. The placard on the left reads 'I am the biggest sow in town. I never on the Jew boys frown!' The placard the man is holding reads 'As a Jew, I only take German girls to my room'.

ACTIVITY ?

What does Source A tell you about attitudes to the Jews in Nazi Germany?

101

Jews and Slavs, on the other hand, were believed by the Nazis to be *Untermenschen* or 'subhumans'. Nazi propaganda portrayed Jews as evil moneylenders. Hitler wished to drive the Slavs out of Eastern Europe so that he could secure more land for Germany (*Lebensraum*, see page 35). He would enslave any who remained, though he did think that a few might be 'Germanised'. He began to carry out this policy after 1939, when the war started. Hitler regarded the Jews as an evil force and was convinced of their involvement in a world conspiracy to destroy civilisation. Hitler wanted to portray the Jews as a wandering race of people who had, over the centuries, infiltrated all aspects of civilised society and had to be removed (see Source B).

> **Source B** From a speech given by Hitler in 1922
>
> There can be no compromise. There are only two possibilities: either victory of the Aryan master race, or the wiping out of the Aryan and the victory of the Jew.

Practice question

Give two things you can infer from Source B about Hitler's attitude towards the Jews. *(For guidance, see page 78.)*

ACTIVITY ?

What message does Source C give about the Jews?

Source C A poster from an exhibition, used by the Nazis to turn people against the Jews, with the caption 'The Eternal Jew'. The image of the hammer and sickle under the left arm of the figure were symbols of the Soviet Union

GROSSE POLITISCHE SCHAU IM BIBLIOTHEKSBAU DES DEUTSCHEN MUSEUMS ZU MÜNCHEN · AB 8. NOVEMBER 1937 · TÄGLICH GEÖFFNET VON 10-21 UHR

13.2 The persecution of the Jews

Hitler and the Nazi Party were by no means the first to think of the Jews as different and to treat them with hostility as outsiders. **Anti-Semitism** goes back to the Middle Ages.

Jewish people have been persecuted throughout history, for example in England during the Middle Ages. This is because Jewish people stood out as different in regions across Europe. They had a different religion and different customs. Some Christians blamed the Jews for the execution of Christ and argued that Jews should be punished forever. Some Jews became moneylenders and became quite wealthy. This increased resentment and suspicion from people who owed them money or were jealous of their success.

Why were the Jews persecuted?

Hitler had spent several years in Vienna where there was a long tradition of anti-Semitism.

He lived as a down and out and resented the wealth of many of the Viennese Jews. In the 1920s he used the Jews as scapegoats for all society's problems.

He blamed them for Germany's defeat in the First World War, hyperinflation in 1923 and the Depression of 1929.

Hitler was determined to create a 'pure' racial state. This did not include the 500,000 Jews who were living in Germany. He wanted to eliminate the Jews from German society. He had no master plan for achieving this, however, and until the beginning of the Second World War; a great deal of Nazi Jewish policy was uncoordinated.

◀ **Source D** A Nazi cartoon with the title 'Jewish department store octopus'

ACTIVITIES ?

1 What is the message of the cartoon in Source D? How does it show one reason why the Nazis persecuted the Jews?

2 Give two reasons why Hitler decided to persecute the Jews.

How did the lives of German Jews change in the years 1933–39?

The persecution of the Jews did not begin immediately. Hitler needed to ensure that he had the support of most of the German people for his anti-Semitic policies. This was achieved through propaganda and the use of schools. Young people especially were encouraged to hate Jews, with school lessons and textbooks putting across anti-Semitic views.

School textbooks and teaching materials were controlled by the government Ministry of Education (see page 91). The government was able to put anti-Semitic material into every classroom. In addition, laws were passed to restrict the role of education for Jewish people. In October 1936, Jewish teachers were forbidden to give private tuition to German students. In November 1938, Jewish children were expelled from German schools.

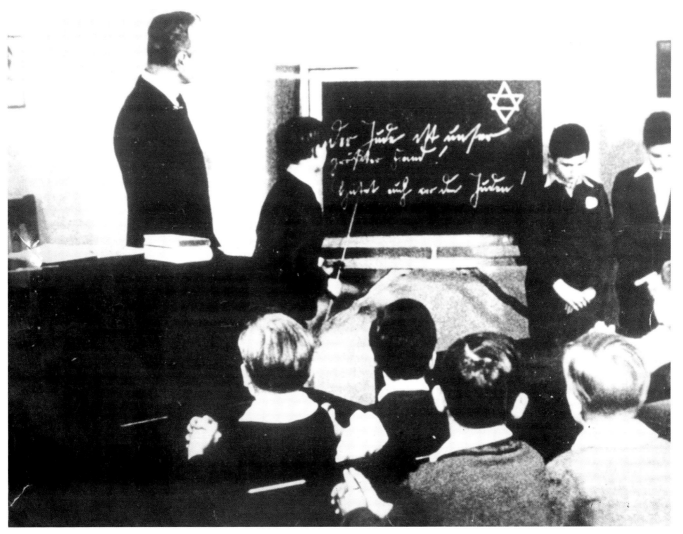

▲ **Source E** Two Jewish schoolchildren being humiliated in front of their class in 1935. The writing on the blackboard translates to 'The Jew is our greatest enemy. Beware of the Jews!'

„Die Judennaſe iſt an ihrer Spitze gebogen. Sie ſieht aus wie ein Sechſer…"

▲ **Source F** This picture shows a page from an anti-Semitic children's book. The text reads, 'The Jewish nose is crooked at its tip. It looks like the number 6.'

Source G From the memoirs of a German mother, written after the Second World War

One day my daughter came home humiliated. 'It was not so nice today.' 'What happened?' I asked. The teacher had sent the Aryan children to one side of the classroom, and the non-Aryans to the other. Then the teacher told the Aryans to study the appearance of the others and to point out the marks of their Jewish race. They stood separated as if by a gulf, children who had played together as friends the day before.

Source H Extract from a school textbook

Inge sits in the doctor's waiting room. Again and again her mind dwells on the warnings of the BDM leader: 'A German must not consult a Jewish doctor! And particularly not a German girl! Many a girl who has gone to a Jewish doctor to be cured has found disease and disgrace.

The door opens. Inge looks in. There stands the Jew. She screams. She's so frightened she drops the magazine. Her eyes stare into the Jewish doctor's face. His face is the face of the devil. In the middle of the devil's face is a huge crooked nose. Behind the spectacles two criminal eyes. And thick lips that are grinning. 'Now, I've got you at last, a little German girl.'

▲ **Source I** An illustration from a children's book, warning children not to trust Jews

ACTIVITIES

1 Study Sources E and G. What do these sources show about the treatment of Jews under the Nazis? Explain your answer.
2 Study Source F. Why would this be used in Nazi schools?
3 Study Source H. What message is it trying to get across? How does it put across this message?
4 Study Source I. How does the artist turn German people against the Jews?
5 Explain the effects of Nazi racial policies on German schoolchildren in Nazi Germany in the years 1933–39.

The boycott of Jewish shops, April 1933

Almost as soon as he had become Chancellor, Hitler began to take steps against the Jews. Germans were persuaded to boycott Jewish shops and businesses. The boycott was a reaction to stories in the international press which criticised the new Nazi regime. The Nazis claimed that these stories were instigated by Jews living abroad.

The boycott began on Saturday, 1 April, and lasted only a day. Members of the SA placed themselves at entrances to Jewish shops, department stores and other places of business, discouraging entry. The SA painted the Star of David on many of the shops' doors and windows. The police rarely stopped the SA even when there were acts of physical violence.

However, most Germans ignored the boycott. Moreover, the day was a Saturday, the Jewish Sabbath, and many Jewish shops were closed.

Source J The SA-enforced ▶ boycott of Jewish shops in April 1933

Source K Martha Dodd, the daughter of the US Ambassador in Germany, writing in *My Years in Germany*, in 1939

As we were coming out of the hotel we saw a crowd gathering in the middle of the street. We stopped to find out what it was all about. There was a tram in the middle of the road from which a young girl was being brutally pushed and shoved. She looked terrible. Her head had been shaved clean of hair and she was wearing a placard across her chest. The placard said: 'I have offered myself to the Jews'.

ACTIVITY ?

Study Source K. Why do you think the woman was treated this way?

The Nuremberg Laws, 1935

On 15 September 1935, the Nazi government passed two new racial laws at their annual Reich Party Congress in Nuremberg, Germany. These two laws (the Reich Citizenship Law and the Law to Protect German Blood and Honour) became known as the Nuremberg Laws. The Reich Citizenship Law stated that only those of German blood could be German citizens. Jews lost their citizenship, the right to vote and hold government office. By removing their civil rights, the Nazis had legally pushed Jews to the edges of society.

The Law for the Protection of German Blood and Honour forbade marriage or sexual relations between Jews and German citizens. Marriages that had occurred before this law were still classed as legal but German citizens were encouraged to divorce their existing Jewish partners. Few did so.

> **Source L** The Reich Citizenship Law, 1935
>
> Only a national of Germany or similar blood, who proves by his behaviour that he is willing and able loyally to serve the German people and Reich is a citizen of the Reich. A Jew may not be a citizen of the Reich. He has no vote. He may not hold any public office.

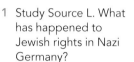

ACTIVITIES

1 Study Source L. What has happened to Jewish rights in Nazi Germany?

2 Imagine you are a Jewish teenager who kept a diary during the 1930s. Write three to five entries explaining your feelings about Nazi policies. For example, your reactions to the boycott of Jewish shops, your treatment at school and the Nuremberg Laws.

Practice questions

1 Give two things you can infer from Source L about the treatment of the Jews in Nazi Germany. (*For guidance, see page 78.*)

2 How useful are Sources J and L for an enquiry into the treatment of the Jews in Nazi Germany? Explain your answer, using Sources J and L and your knowledge of the historical context. (*For guidance, see pages 62–64.*)

◀ **Source M** A sign which reads 'Jews are not wanted in this area', 1933

Kristallnacht, 9 November 1938

After a brief easing of persecution during the 1936 Olympic Games, the persecution of the Jews began to grow and worsened especially after the *Anschluss* with Austria in March 1938. Then in November there was a violent outburst of anti-Semitism in Germany.

On 8 November 1938 a young Polish Jew, Herschel Grynszpan, walked into the German Embassy in Paris and shot the first official he met. He was protesting against the treatment of his parents, who had been deported from Germany to Poland. Goebbels used this as an opportunity to organise anti-Jewish demonstrations which involved attacks on Jewish property, shops, homes and synagogues. So many windows were smashed in the campaign that the events of 9–10 November became known as Kristallnacht, meaning 'Crystal Night' or 'the Night of Broken Glass'. About 100 Jews were killed and 20,000 sent to concentration camps. About 7,500 Jewish businesses were destroyed.

The Nazi government did not permit Jewish property owners to make any insurance claims for damage to property. In addition, any surviving Jewish businesses were not allowed to re-open under Jewish management, but had to have 'pure' Germans in charge of them.

Many Germans were disgusted by Kristallnacht. Hitler and Goebbels were anxious that it should not be seen as the work of the Nazis. It was portrayed as a spontaneous act of vengeance by Germans. In all, 191 synagogues were destroyed together with 815 Jewish businesses.

Source N A US official describes what he saw in Leipzig

The shattering of shop windows, looting of stores and dwellings of Jews took place in the early hours of 10 November 1938. In one of the Jewish sections an eighteen-year-old boy was hurled from a three-storey window to land with both legs broken on a street littered with broken beds. The main streets of the city were a positive litter of shattered glass. All the synagogues were gutted by flames.

ACTIVITIES

1 What can you learn from Source N about Kristallnacht?

2 In what ways does the German newspaper article in *Der Stürmer* differ from the views expressed by *The Daily Telegraph*?

3 How seriously did the following measures threaten the position of Jews in Nazi Germany? Make a copy of the following table and give a brief explanation for your decisions.

Event	Rating 1–10 (10 is very serious)	Reason
Boycott of Jewish shops, 1933		
Nuremberg Laws, 1935		
Kristallnacht, 1938		

The Daily Telegraph
12 November 1938

Mob law rules

Mob law ruled in Berlin throughout the afternoon and evening as hordes of hooligans took part in an orgy of destruction. I have never seen an anti-Jewish outbreak as sickening as this. I saw fashionably dressed women clapping their hands and screaming with glee while respectable mothers held up their babies to see the 'fun'. No attempt was made by the police to stop the rioters.

Der Stürmer
10 November 1938

Revenge for murder by a Jew

The death of a loyal party member by the Jewish murderer has aroused spontaneous anti-Jewish demonstrations throughout the Reich. In many places Jewish shops have been smashed. The synagogues, from which teachings hostile to the State and People are spread, have been set on fire. Well done to those Germans who have ensured revenge for the murder of an innocent German.

▲ **Source O** A Jewish shop in Berlin the day after Kristallnacht

The aftermath

Hitler officially blamed the Jews themselves for having provoked the attacks and used this as an excuse to step up the campaign against them. He decreed the following:

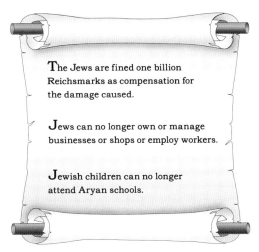

The Jews are fined one billion Reichsmarks as compensation for the damage caused.

Jews can no longer own or manage businesses or shops or employ workers.

Jewish children can no longer attend Aryan schools.

The persecution continued in 1939.

- In January the Reich Office for Jewish Emigration was established. Reinhard Heydrich was its director. The SS became responsibile for driving the Jews from Germany. This would be achieved by forced emigration.

- In the following months Jews were required to surrender precious metals and jewellery.
- On 30 April Jews were evicted from their homes and forced into designated Jewish accommodation or ghettos.
- In September Jews were forced to hand in their radio sets so they could not listen to foreign news.
- By the summer of 1939, about 250,000 Jews had left Germany.

Practice question

Explain why there were changes to the lives of Jewish people in Nazi Germany in the years 1933–39.

You may use the following in your answer:
- The Nuremburg Laws, 1935
- Kristallnacht, 1938

You must also use information of your own.

(For guidance, see pages 94–95)

Measures taken against the Jews

As we have seen, persecution of the Jews in the 1930s was irregular. Initially there was the economic boycott, which was not well supported and disliked by many Germans. Then legal and open discrimination increased in the years to 1936 but diminished during the Olympics. Persecution then increased with further legislation and Kristallnacht. Increased numbers of Jews had left Germany by the end of the decade. The diagram below summarises the different measures

1933	April	The SA organised a boycott of Jewish shops and businesses. They painted *Jude* (Jew) on windows and tried to persuade the public not to enter. Thousands of Jewish civil servants, lawyers and university teachers were sacked.
	May	A new law excluded Jews from government jobs. Jewish books were burnt.
	September	Jews were banned from inheriting land.

| 1934 | | Local councils banned Jews from public spaces such as parks, playing fields and swimming pools. |

1935	May	Jews were no longer drafted into the army.
	June	Restaurants were closed to Jews all over Germany.
	September	The Nuremberg Laws (see page 107) a series of measures aimed against Jews, were passed on 15 September.

| 1936 | April | The professional activities of Jews were banned or restricted – this included vets, dentists, accountants, surveyors, teachers and nurses. |
| | July–August | There was a deliberate lull in the anti-Jewish campaign as Germany was hosting the Olympics (see page 77) and wanted to give the outside world a good impression. |

| 1937 | September | For the first time in two years Hitler publicly attacked the Jews. More and more Jewish businesses were taken over. |

1938	March	Jews had to register their possessions, making it easier to confiscate them.
	July	Jews had to carry identity cards. Jewish doctors, dentists and lawyers were forbidden to treat Aryans.
	August	Jewish men had to add the name 'Israel' to their first names, Jewish women the name 'Sarah', to further humiliate them.
	October	Jews had the red letter 'J' stamped on their passports.
	November	Kristallnacht (see page 108). Young Jews were excluded from schools and universities.

ACTIVITIES

1 Make a copy of the table below and give examples of measures which removed Jews' political, social or economic rights. One example has been done for you.

Political	
Economic	Boycott of shops
Social	

2 Using a flow diagram, show the key changes in the lives of Jews in Germany 1933–39.

13.3 The treatment of minorities

Ideal Germans were 'socially useful' in that they had a job and contributed to the state. Anyone else was seen as a 'burden on the community'. These included those who could not work, the unhealthy, mentally disabled, tramps and beggars. The term used to describe them was 'asocial'. The Nazis considered these people worthless and expensive to the state and they had to be removed because they could not contribute to the *Volksgemeinschaft*.

There were also socially undesirable groups such as alcoholics, homosexuals and juvenile delinquents. They were also seen as dangerous and a bad influence on others. Once again, they had to be removed from society.

As they had with the Jews, the Nazis began with a propaganda campaign to ensure that most German people turned against these undesirable groups. This propaganda was followed by more extreme measures, as shown in the boxes below.

STERILISATION LAW

This law was passed in July 1933. It allowed the Nazis to sterilise people with certain illnesses, such as 'simple-mindedness' and 'chronic alcoholism'. Between 1934 and 1945 about 350,000 people were compulsorily sterilised.

CONCENTRATION CAMPS

Many 'undesirables' were sent to **concentration camps** (see pages 67–68), including prostitutes, homosexual people and juvenile delinquents. In 1938, **Gypsies**, vagrants and beggars were added to the list.

EUTHANASIA CAMPAIGN

In 1939, the Nazis secretly began to exterminate the mentally ill in a **euthanasia** campaign. The mentally ill were seen as a threat to Aryan purity. Around 6,000 disabled babies, children and teenagers were murdered by starvation or lethal injection.

People with disabilities

In their pursuit of a perfect race, the Nazis passed the Sterilisation Law. This law enabled them to sterilise people who suffered from physical deformity, mental illness, epilepsy, learning disabilities, blindness and deafness. Those who were physically disabled were called 'unworthy of life' or 'useless eaters' and were called a burden upon society.

> **Source P** Commentary from a 1937 Nazi film
>
> Sterilisation is a simple surgical operation. In the last 70 years our people have increased by 50 per cent while in the same period the number of hereditary ill has risen by over 450 per cent. If this was to continue, there would be one hereditary ill person to four healthy people. An endless column of horror would march into the nation.

Homosexual people

The Nazis' views about the importance of family life and producing children meant that same-sex relationships could not be tolerated. The Nazis were no different to the rest of Europe and did not look favourably on homosexuality and maintained its illegal status. Gay men were arrested and sent to concentration camps. Lesbians were not seen as a threat to the Nazi state and were not persecuted in such a way because they were seen to be passive and subordinate to men.

The Gypsies

There were about 30,000 Gypsies in Germany at the time. The Nazis gave two reasons for removing them:

- They were non-Aryan and threatened racial purity.
- They were people who travelled across the country and had no fixed home, and thus threatened the Nazi view of stable family life. The Nazis also accused them of being 'work-shy'.

In 1935, the Nazis banned all marriages between Gypsies and Germans. Three years later a decree for the 'struggle against the gypsy plague' was issued. All Gypsies had to register with the authorities.

> **Source Q** From a letter to a Frankfurt newspaper from some citizens about the 'Gypsy nuisance'
>
> Right opposite properties Gypsies have settled themselves. They are a heavy burden on the community. The hygienic conditions in this area defy description. We are worried about the spread of contagious diseases. Because of the Gypsies our properties have greatly fallen in value.

ACTIVITIES

1. What reason is given for sterilisation in Source P?
2. Study Source Q. Why were some Germans opposed to Gypsies?
3. Explain why minority groups were targeted by the Nazis.

Revise and practise

Key topic 1

1 The origins of the Republic, 1918–19

1 Place the following events in chronological order:
- ☐ Prince Max of Baden formed new government
- ☐ Armistice signed
- ☐ Kaiser Wilhelm abdicated
- ☐ Kiel Mutiny
- ☐ Ebert new Chancellor
- ☐ USA joined the war

2 Match the definitions to the terms.

Terms:	Definitions:
■ The Fourteen Points	■ The 'stab in the back' theory
■ *Dolchstoss*	■ The number of election votes won determined the number of seats in the Reichstag
■ Proportional representation	■ Two or more parties
■ Coalition government	■ Measures taken by the president in an emergency
■ Article 48	■ The principles laid down by President Wilson at Versailles

2 The early challenges to the Weimar Republic, 1919–23

1 Explain, in no more than two sentences, what you know about the following:
- a) Article 231 of the Treaty of Versailles
- b) *Diktat*
- c) Reparations
- d) Spartacists
- e) *Freikorps*
- f) *Reichswehr*
- g) The Kapp Putsch

2 Summarise in 25 words or fewer the following problems faced by the Weimar government:

Proportional representation	
Hyperinflation	
Treaty of Versailles	
French occupation of the Ruhr	

3 The recovery of the Republic, 1924–29

1 Using a circular diagram like the one below, categorise the importance of the following reasons for the recovery of Germany in the years 1924–29, beginning with the most important in the centre to the least important on the outside.
- ☐ Dawes Plan
- ☐ Stresemann
- ☐ Rentenmark
- ☐ US loans

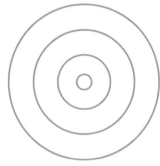

2 Which of these statements best sums up the period of recovery? Give reasons for your decision.
- ☐ It provided strong foundations for future economic growth.
- ☐ Germany was left too dependent on the US economy.
- ☐ All sectors of the economy prospered in these years.

4 Changes in society, 1924–29

1 Are the following statements about the Weimar Republic in the years 1924–29 true or false?

Statement	True	False
Real wages decreased in these years.		
Two million new houses were built.		
Women over 18 were given the vote in 1918.		
By 1933 one-tenth of members of the Reichstag were female.		
One of the most famous artists of the period was Bertolt Brecht.		

2 What is meant by the following terms?
- ☐ *Zeittheater* and *Zeitoper*
- ☐ Bauhaus
- ☐ *Neue Sachlichkeit*

Key topic 2

5 The development of the Nazi Party, 1920–29

1 Place the following events in Hitler's life in chronological order:
☐ Hitler jailed
☐ Day of birth
☐ Death of his mother
☐ Hitler became leader of the NSDAP
☐ Munich Putsch
☐ Death of his father
☐ Left Vienna to live in Munich
☐ Joined DAP

2 Write three sentences to explain why the following were important to the Nazi Party in the years to 1923–29:
☐ The *Sturmabteilung*
☐ *Führerprinzip*
☐ Hyperinflation
☐ Twenty-Five Point Programme
☐ The Munich Putsch
☐ *Mein Kampf*

3 What explanation can you give for the following statements?
☐ Hitler's trial was excellent publicity for Hitler.
☐ Imprisonment was beneficial for Hitler.

4 Who or what were the following:
a) The *Bürgerbräukeller*
b) General Ludendorff
c) Landberg Prison
d) *Volksgemeinschaft*
e) *Lebensraum*

6 The growth in support for the Nazis, 1929–33

1 Write one sentence to explain why each of the following was important in the Depression:
☐ Ending the Dawes Plan
☐ Death of Stresemann
☐ Article 48
☐ Shortage of food
☐ Banks collapse

2 Are the following statements about the Nazis' election methods during the years 1930–32 true or false?

Statement	True	False
They advertised on television.		
They used huge numbers of posters across Germany.		
They only used violence in order to defend themselves.		
They used modern technology.		
Hitler kept his message simple.		

3 Make a copy of the following grid and give at least three reasons in each column to show how each helped Hitler to come to power.

Treaty of Versailles	The Great Depression	Political intrigue

4 Write a paragraph on each of the following two statements, explaining why you agree with it.
a) Hitler's own personal attraction and speaking ability were the main reasons why he won the support of the people.
b) Fear of Communism in Germany was the main reason Hitler won the support of many people.

Key topic 3

7 The creation of a dictatorship, 1933–34

1 Write two or three sentences that agree with the following statement.
   ☐ The Reichstag fire was a Communist plot.

2 Make a copy of the following grid and in fifteen words or fewer summarise why each was important for the Nazis.

The SA	
Enabling Law	
Support of the army	
Death of Hindenburg	

3 Decide whether the following statements are causes or effects of the Night of the Long Knives.

Statement	Cause	Effect
Hitler needed the support of the army.		
Röhm was too powerful.		
The SS and Gestapo became stronger.		
Terror grew.		
The SA wanted a social revolution.		
Hitler had fewer opponents.		
Röhm wanted to lead all the armed forces.		

8 Controlling and influencing attitudes

1 Explain why the following were important in the creation of a Nazi police state:
   ☐ Gestapo
   ☐ SS
   ☐ The People's Court
   ☐ Concentration camps

2 Pair together the following sentences.
   a) A great many Protestants refused to support the Nazis.
   b) Hitler soon broke his agreement with the Pope.
   c) Some Protestants, led by Pastor Ludwig Müller, supported the Nazis.
   i) They set up the 'German Christians'.
   ii) They were led by Pastor Niemöller and set up the German Confessional Church.
   iii) He began to persecute the Catholic Church by closing their schools and youth movements.

3 Using illustrations only, show the meaning of
   ☐ Censorship
   ☐ Propaganda

4 Make a copy of the following grid and in no more than ten words summarise Nazi cultural changes.

	Change
Art	
Architecture	
Music	
Theatre	
Films	
Sport	

5 The following account of Nazi propaganda is by a student who has not revised thoroughly. Re-write the account, correcting any errors.

   In 1933, Hermann Goering was made Minister of Propaganda. He organised a massive annual rally at a place called Stuttgart. In May 1933, students and members of the SA organised a mass book burning. They mainly burnt copies of Mein Kampf. Expensive radios were produced so that only a few Germans could hear Nazi broadcasts.

9 Opposition, resistance and conformity in Nazi Germany

Explain, in no more than two sentences, what you know about the opposition of the following to Hitler and the Nazi regime:

- The Edelweiss Pirates
- The Swing Youth
- Pastor Niemöller
- The Catholic Church

Key topic 4

10 Nazi policies towards women

1 Choose one of the following interpretations of women in Nazi Germany and write a paragraph justifying the statement.
   - ☐ There was considerable change in the position of women under the Nazis.
   - ☐ There was some change in the position of women under the Nazis.
   - ☐ There was little change in the position of women under the Nazis.

2 Make a copy of the following table and, using key words, summarise the main differences between the role of women before and after 1933.

	Before 1933	After 1933
Marriage and children		
Work		

11 Nazi policies towards the young

1 Are the following statements about Hitler's policies towards the young true or false?

Statement	True	False
Boys and girls were taught in separate schools.		
Children joined the Hitler Youth at the age of eight.		
Very little PE was taught in schools.		
At the age of fourteen girls joined the League of German Girls.		
Teachers had to join the Nazi Teachers' League.		

2 Explain, in no more than a sentence, what you know about the following:
   - ☐ The *Deutsches Jungvolk*
   - ☐ Physical education
   - ☐ Hitler Youth activities
   - ☐ Nazi Teachers' League
   - ☐ School curriculum

12 Employment and living standards

1 What were the following?
   - a) Beauty of Work
   - b) Strength through Joy
   - c) The Labour Front
   - d) Labour Service
   - e) The Volkswagen scheme

2 Were the German workers better off under the Nazis? Fill in a Venn diagram, with labels 'Evidence that they were better off' on the left circle, 'No change' where the circles intersect, and 'Evidence that they were worse off' on the right circle.

3 What explanation can you give for the following contradictory statements?
   - ☐ The Nazis wanted to reduce the number of women working, yet there were more employed in 1939 than in 1933.
   - ☐ Workers' wages were higher in 1939 than in 1933, yet they were worse off moneywise.
   - ☐ Many Jews and women lost their jobs after 1933, yet unemployment figures went down.

13 The persecution of minorities

1 Summarise in no more than ten words these examples of the treatment of the Jews:
   - ☐ Kristallnacht
   - ☐ The Nuremberg Laws
   - ☐ Boycott of Jewish shops
   - ☐ Local councils
   - ☐ Forenames

2 Place these events in chronological order:
   - ☐ Kristallnacht
   - ☐ Boycott of Jewish shops
   - ☐ The Nuremberg Laws
   - ☐ Local councils banning Jews in public places

3 Match the words to the definitions.

Words:
   - ☐ euthanasia
   - ☐ anti-Semitism
   - ☐ Aryan
   - ☐ subhuman

Definitions:
   - ☐ Hatred of or policies against the Jews
   - ☐ Tall, blond and blue-eyed
   - ☐ According to the Nazis, members of the underclass such as Jews and Slavs
   - ☐ Act of killing someone to relieve suffering

Glossary

Anschluss   The annexation of Austria by Germany in 1938

Anti-Semitism   Hatred and persecution of the Jews

Armistice   The ending of hostilities in a war

Aryan   Nazi term for a non-Jewish German, someone of supposedly 'pure' German stock

Bolshevism   Named from the Bolsheviks, members of the Russian Social Democrat Workers Party, who followed Lenin

Bolshevik revolution   A revolution in Russia in 1917–18 that overthrew the tsar and brought the Bolsheviks to power

Capitalism   An economic system in which the production and distribution of goods depend on private investment

Censorship   Controlling what is produced and suppressing anything considered to be against the state

Centre Party (ZP)   A Catholic party occupying the middle ground in political views

Civil rights   Basic rights of citizens such as the right to vote, equal treatment under the law, etc.

Coalition government   A government of two or more political parties

Communist Party (KPD)   The German Communist Party, following the ideas of Karl Marx

Communists   Followers of the communist ideas of Karl Marx, who believed, for example, that the state should own the means of production and distribution

Concentration camp   Prison for political prisoners and enemies of the state, who are placed there without trial

Concordat   An agreement between the Pope and a government concerning the legal status of the Roman Catholic Church within that government's territory

Conscription   Compulsory military service for a certain period of time

Constitution   The basic principles according to which a country is governed

DAP (*Deutsche Arbeiterpartei*)   The German Workers' Party

Dawes Plan   Introduced in 1924 to restructure Germany's annual reparation payments

DDP (German Democratic Party)   A left-wing liberal party founded in 1918

DNVP (*Deutschnationale Volkspartei*)   The German National People's Party, the nationalist right-wing party supported by business people and landowners

Dolchstoss   'Stab in the back'

Enabling Act   The law that gave Hitler the power to rule for four years without consulting the Reichstag

Euthanasia   Bringing death to relieve suffering. The Nazis interpreted this as killing anyone who was seen as substandard and of no further use to the state

Federal structure   System in which power is divided between a central government (Reichstag) and regional governments (*Länder*)

Fourteen Points   The principles laid down by President Wilson as the war aims of the USA

Freikorps   Private armies set up by senior German army officers at the end of the First World War. Mainly comprised ex-soldiers

Führerprinzip   The leadership principle; the idea that the Nazi Party and Germany should have one leader, obeyed by all

German Faith Movement   Religious movement that sought to move Germany away from Christianity. It put forward the Nazi idea of 'blood and soil', the cult of Hitler and pagan ideas such as sun worship

German Labour Front (DAF)   Organisation set up by the Nazis to control German workers

Gestapo (*Geheime Staatspolizei*)   Official secret police of the Nazi regime

Ghetto   A densely populated area of a city inhabited by a particular ethnic group, such as Jews

Gleichschaltung   Bringing people into an identical way of thinking and behaving

Great Depression   Slump in the economy in the 1930s which led to high unemployment

Gypsy   A race of people found across Europe who generally travel across the continent rather than living in one place

Heil Hitler   Form of salute to Hitler

Hitler Youth   Organisation set up for the young in Germany to convert them to Nazi ideas

Hyperinflation   Extremely high inflation, where the value of money plummets and it becomes almost worthless

Indoctrination   Converting people to your ideas using education and propaganda

Informant   Person who gives information to the authorities about the activities of other people

Kaiser   The German emperor

Länder   Regional states of Germany

League of Nations   The international body established after the First World War in order to maintain peace

Left wing Of politicians and parties which favour socialism

Manifesto A public declaration of a political party's policies

Minister without Portfolio A minister of state who is not appointed to any specific department in a government

National Socialist Member of the NSDAP

Nationalise To change from private ownership to state ownership

Nationalist Party Shortened form of the German National People's Party (DNVP)

Nazi-Nationalist government Coalition of NSDAP and DNVP after January 1933

Nazi Teachers' League Organisation set up to control teachers and what they taught

November Criminals Name given to the German politicians who accepted the armistice which ended the First World War

Passive resistance Opposition to a government, invading power, etc., without using violence

Plebiscite Direct vote of the electorate on an important public issue

Proportional representation The number of votes won in an election, determined the number of seats in the Reichstag

Purge Removal of opponents

Putsch Attempted takeover of the government

Reich In German, this has many meanings – state, kingdom, empire. When used by the Nazis it tended to mean empire or Germany

Reichsbank German National Bank

Reichstag German state parliament

Reichswehr German army and navy

Reparations War damages (money) to be paid by Germany

Republic A state in which the government is carried out by the people or their elected representatives

SA (*Sturmabteilung*) The paramilitary 'storm troopers' of the Nazi Party

Scapegoat A person or group made to take the blame for others

SD (*Sicherheitsdienst*) 'security service', the intelligence agency of the Nazis

Slavs Eastern Europeans including Polish and Russians

Social Democratic Party (SPD) Main left-wing party, supported mainly by the working class

Socialists Those who believe in state ownership

SS (*Schutzstaffel*) Orignally the Nazi paramilitary organisation that acted as Hitler's bodyguard, they became the most powerful troops in the the Third Reich and carried out the Final Solution

Swastika Emblem of the Nazi Party; a cross with the arms bent at right angles

Third Reich Nazi name for Germany. Means 'Third Empire'

Thousand Year Reich Another name for the Third Reich. Hitler proclaimed that the Nazi era would last for a thousand years

Trade unions Organisations set up to protect and improve the rights of workers

Treason A crime committed against the state

Völkisch Literally 'of the people'. In Germany it grew to mean being linked to extreme German nationalism and Germanic racial awareness

Volksgemeinschaft The people's community. This was the Nazi idea of a community based upon the German race

Wall Street Crash 29 October 1929, when more than 16 million shares were traded in panic selling, triggering further sales and leading to a world economic crisis

Weimar Republic The republic that existed in Germany from 1919 to 1933

Index

Acknowledgements

Photo credits

The Publishers would like to thank the following for permission to reproduce copyright material.

Pages 6 & 17 (left) © World History Archive/TopFoto; **p.7** ©Hulton Archive/Getty Images; **p.8** © Scherl/Süddeutsche Zeitung Photo; **p.14** © Stapleton Historical Collection/ HIP/TopFoto; **p.15** © ullstein bild via Getty Images; **p.17** (right) © ullstein bild/ TopFoto; **p.20** © IMAGNO/Austrian Archives/TopFoto; **p.22** © Imagno/Getty Images; **p.25** © Scherl/Süddeutsche Zeitung Photo; **p.26** © Estate of George Grosz, Princeton, NJ/ DACS, 2015/Nationalegalerie, SMB/Jörg P.Anders/bpk; **p.28** © Scherl/Süddeutsche Zeitung Photo; **p.29** © Hulton Archive/Getty Images; **p.30** © Friedrich/Interfoto/ akg-images; **p.33** © Heinrich Hoffmann/ullstein bild/Getty Images; **p.34** © dpa dena/ dpa/Corbis; **p.36** © Scherl/Süddeutsche Zeitung Photo; **p.40** © Walter Ballhause/akg-images; **p.41** © ullsteinbild/TopFoto; **p.42** (left) © ullsteinbild/TopFoto, (right) © Walter Frentz/ullstein bild; **p.44** (left) © R.Feltz/TopFoto, (right) © Randall Bytwerk (http:// research.calvin.edu/german-propaganda-archive); **p.45** (top) © Universal History Archive/Getty Images, (bottom) © The Heartfield Community of Heirs/VG Bild-Kunst, Bonn and DACS, London 2015/akg-images; **p.46** (top) © Scherl/Süddeutsche Zeitung Photo, (bottom) © INTERFOTO/Alamy Stock Photo; **p.47** © Hulton Archive/Getty Images; **p.48** © The Print Collector/Print Collector/Getty Images; **p.49** © TopFoto; **p.50** (left) © ullsteinbild/TopFoto, (right) © Punch Limited; **pp.53 & 75** (left) © Topfoto; **p.54** © Topfoto; **p.55** (left) © Bettmann/Corbis, (right) © Bettmann/Corbis; **p.57** © akg-images; **p.58** © Bettmann/Corbis; **p.60** (top) Cartoon by David Low: 'They salute with both hands now.' © David Low/Solo Syndication. Photo courtesy of British Cartoon Archive, University of Kent, www.cartoons.ac.uk, (bottom) © Strube/Express Newspapers/ N&S Syndication. Photo courtesy of British Cartoon Archive, University of Kent, www. cartoons.ac.uk; **p.61** (top) © Hulton Archive/Getty Images, (bottom) © Imagno/Getty Images; **p.65** © Topfoto; **p.66** © Corbis; **p.68** © akg-images/ullstein bild; **p.69** © bpk; **p.72** (left) © akg-images, (right) © The Heartfield Community of Heirs/VG Bild-Kunst, Bonn and DACS, London 2015; **p.73** © Hugo Jaeger/Timepix/The LIFE Picture Collection/Getty Images; **p.74** © Mary Evans Picture Library/Alamy Stock Photo; **p.75** (right) © ullstein bild/Getty Images; **p.76** © Mary Evans Picture Library/Alamy Stock Photo; **p.77** © Getty Images; **p.81** (top) © Universal History Archive/Getty Images; (bottom) Photo courtesy of Jazzinstitut Darmstadt; **p.82** © bpk; **p.83** © Fine Art Images/HIP/TopFoto; **p.85** © The Granger Collection/Topfoto; **p.86** © The Wiener Library; **p.87** © akg-images; **p.88** (left) Courtesy of Hoover Institution Library & Archives, Stanford University (Foto-Willinger collection, Envelope CP), (right) © ullsteinbild/TopFoto; **p.92** (left) © akg-images, (right) © ullsteinbild/TopFoto; **p.93** (top) © Knorr + Hirth/Süddeutsche Zeitung Photo, (bottom) © akg-images; **p.96** © ullsteinbild/TopFoto; **p.97** (top) © ullstein bild/Getty Images, (bottom) © akg-images; **p.98** © akg-images; **p.99** © Scherl/Süddeutsche Zeitung Photo; **p.101** © Keystone/Getty Images; **p.102** © akg-images; **p.103** © WEIMAR ARCHIVE/ Mary Evans Picture Library; **p.104** © Topfoto; **p.105** (left) © Deutsches Historisches Museum, Berlin, (right) Photo courtesy United States Holocaust Memorial Museum; **p.106** © akg-images; **p.107** © Bildarchiv Pisarek/akg-images; **p.109** © World History Archive/TopFoto.

Every effort has been made to trace all copyright holders, but if any have been inadvertently overlooked, the Publishers will be pleased to make the necessary arrangements at the first opportunity.